YESTERDAY'S WORLD

TOMORROW'S LANDSCAPE

The English Heritage
Historic Landscape Project 1992–94

ENGLISH HERITAGE

YESTERDAY'S WORLD
TOMORROW'S LANDSCAPE

The English Heritage
Historic Landscape Project 1992–94

Graham Fairclough, George Lambrick, Andrew McNab

With contributions by:

Paul Chadwick; David Freke; Mark Gardiner; Helen Glass; Peter Herring;
Philip Masters; Julian Munby; Richard Newman; Percival Turnbull

1999

ENGLISH HERITAGE

Copyright © English Heritage 1999
ISBN 1 85074 773 3
Published 1999 by
English Heritage 23 Savile Row,
London W1X 1AB

Editor Graham Fairclough

Production editor Pamela V Irving

Design and layout by Mind's Eye Design, Lewes

Printed by: Laser Graphics Services Limited.

Contents

Illustrations

Tables

Contributors

Paul Chadwick	then Lawson Price, now CgMs Consultants
Graham Fairclough	English Heritage
David Freke	RPS Clouston
Mark Gardiner	South Eastern Archaeological Services
Helen Glass	Chris Blandford Associates
Peter Herring	Cornwall Archaeological Unit
George Lambrick	Oxford Archaeological Unit
Philip Masters	Chris Blandford Associates
Andrew McNab	Cobham Resource Consultants
Julian Munby	Oxford Archaeological Unit
Richard Newman	Lancaster University Archaeological Unit
Percival Turnbull	Archaeological Consultant

Preface

This book describes the results of work carried out between 1992 and 1994 on behalf of English Heritage as part of a widening of its responsibilities for the conservation, preservation, and improved public enjoyment of the historic environment. The approach to historic landscape that it describes takes as its starting point a need to appreciate, and as far as possible understand, the dynamics and historic development of the present-day countryside. Its objective was to develop methods of understanding the landscape in archaeological terms and of assessing its historical value, in order to guide all the day-to-day decisions which continually change the land. Some of these decisions are those of farmers, foresters, and agriculturalists; others are taken by local councils as part of the land use planning system, and still others by national or European government; assessment methods need to be able to influence all of these.

In this work, English Heritage is aware of one overriding principle. The English landscape at the very end of the second millennium AD is the culmination of many thousands of years of human activities and land use. Its valued attributes of variety, patina, or original fitness for purpose all arise from this long succession. While they are valued, however, these attributes are often taken for granted, as if the landscape's historic character was in some way predetermined, timeless, and indeed 'natural'. It is essential that as wide an audience as possible is helped to an awareness that the landscape is a social and cultural construction, an artefact, and that it therefore requires constant maintenance just as any other human artefact does.

It is also, however, a living, evolving, entity, and a starting point for any project of landscape conservation is, therefore, that the landscape's character will be subject inevitably to continued change for both natural and cultural reasons. It cannot be preserved unchanged and its future cannot be taken for granted. Indeed, future change ought not necessarily or automatically to be discouraged. There will be justification for seeking to preserve some elements of the landscape unchanged, for example particularly significant archaeological sites. The goal for the wider landscape however is to seek the creation of new landscape, that encapsulates the old and respects its historic character, in particular by carrying forward the landscape's links with its history. Retaining a sympathy with the past, maintaining critical links and relationships between areas and features, and preserving the broader historic patterns of land use, enclosure, and settlement are all practical objectives within a context of continuing change. The essential first step, however, is understanding, and the main aim of English Heritage's recent work has been to develop a method which can enable the identification of historic landscape character at a broad level, without being carried into too much local detail until the overall picture is clearer.

This approach to landscape conservation aims not to stand in the way of change and

Fig 1: There is a historic dimension even of 'wild' areas: Quernmore, North Lancashire

modernisation, but to inform its detailed direction and its impact on the shape of the future landscape. Change, therefore, has to be well considered and to be guided by knowledge and a proper appreciation of previous generations' legacies. This concern to pass on to future generations an understandable and enjoyable historic landscape is an indispensable contribution to current government interest in achieving sustainable development, preserving and enhancing biodiversity, and, perhaps above all, nurturing local character and fostering quality of life.

The necessary first step for managing the landscape's evolution is to develop robust but appropriate methods of appreciation and understanding. This was the aim of English Heritage's *Historic Landscape Project* in 1992–4, and of methodological development since then. In many ways the project represents merely a first step in a larger programme. It does, however, comprise a discrete phase of the programme and its results are therefore still worth dissemination at this stage. A number of the conclusions have already been taken further in other contexts, and its results are influencing several continuing aspects of the work of English Heritage and local authorities. Indeed, the time which has passed between completion of the project and formal publication of its results has allowed thorough validation and confirmation of its conclusions in several parts of the country, starting with Cornwall, then carried on into other counties (*see Fig 26*). Preliminary descriptions of this later work are contained within this book, notably in chapter 11 and annex 2 (*see also* Fairclough 1999c).

While this report presents a completed and free-standing piece of work, it must nonetheless be read against the wider background of work in progress. Part I gives an introductory overview of the project's origins, in terms of English Heritage's responsibilities and priorities, and attempts to introduce the broad understanding of the term 'historic landscape', which framed the project's work. Part II describes the work of the *Historic Landscape Project* itself, and Part III analyses its results, draws conclusions, and introduces the work already in progress, which has built on the lessons learnt during the research project.

Acknowledgements

Many of the people who helped with this report, or with the work it describes, are also contributors, but most of them made a larger contribution than the chapters reveal. Andrew McNab, Paul Bramhill and Marcus Wood at Cobhams, and George Lambrick carried most of the burden of seeing the project through to a successful conclusion, but in addition I am grateful to Andy Brown, Harriet Jordan and Ken Smith, who were very helpful members of the project Steering Group. I am particularly grateful to colleagues in the Countryside Commission (especially David Brook, Carol Somper, Richard Lloyd and Rosie Simpson) and in English Nature (notably Keith Porter and Rob Cook) for a long series of helpful discussions, while colleagues in other countries of the UK (notably Lesley Macinnes of Cadw and Richard Kelly of the Countryside Commission for Wales) also gave me the benefit of their own ideas and experience. I have also benefited greatly from many discussions at a series of landscape conferences and seminars since *c*1990, with friends and colleagues too numerous to list. Maps, unless otherwise credited are by Central Archaeological Service, English Heritage, while uncredited photographs are by Graham Fairclough. Most of all, however, this books owes it final appearance to Liz Page, who patiently reworked draft after draft as its publication fought for space with other calls on our time.

Graham Fairclough
Sept 1999

PART I: ENGLISH HERITAGE AND THE HISTORIC LANDSCAPE

1: Introduction

Graham Fairclough

Starting points

English Heritage's work on historic landscape had its most immediate origin in *This common inheritance*, the government White Paper published in 1990 (DoE 1990a). This government policy statement reflected the increasingly common view that the historic landscape was receiving insufficient attention in planning circles when compared, for example, to the protection afforded to archaeological sites, historic buildings, or historic parks and gardens. As a first step, in the traditional response to such questions, the White Paper invited English Heritage and the Countryside Commission to consider whether it was desirable to create a register of landscapes of historic significance. A register, or list, of the most special examples of a type of environmental resource is a well-tried and comfortable solution to the problems of conservation, but at a very early stage English Heritage decided that managing the historic landscape requires a more sophisticated and comprehensive treatment. The White Paper invitation was, therefore, taken as an indication of the need for a review of current approaches and practices, and for a study of how most effectively to secure the appropriate management of the landscape's historic dimension. It was not assumed that yet another register would meet that need.

The importance of landscape perspectives in research was further emphasised in *Exploring our past*, English Heritage's 1991 strategy (English Heritage 1991b) for defining research priorities for the 1990's. At the same time, the necessity of taking account of landscape-scale archaeology was becoming apparent with the progress of English Heritage's archaeological evaluation initiative, known as the Monuments Protection Programme (MPP). Scheduling of many monument classes could be progressed relatively successfully on the basis of site comparisons and site evaluations. In several fields, however notably landscape-based historic industry such as lead mining and processing, the crop-mark component of the archaeological resource, and the regional diversity of medieval settlement remains the MPP was being drawn additionally into landscape-level analysis and evaluation which requires different analytical techniques from those applied to conventional site-based evaluation and selection methods.

Fig 2: A landscape characterised by hedgerow patterns, largely post-medieval, in West Shropshire

Basic principles

English Heritage's immediate response to *This common inheritance* was two-fold. A short policy statement was published in June 1991 (Fairclough 1991), and a consultation paper prepared by David Morgan-Evans was issued in October 1991 (English Heritage 1991d). The policy statement was founded on English Heritage's belief that all areas of the country's landscape are historic to some degree, and that the term historic landscape must be taken in its broadest sense to encompass habitats, semi-natural features, hedges, and fields, as well as archaeological sites and buildings. This comprehensive definition of the historic landscape has since received government endorsement in, for example, *Planning policy guidance note 15: planning and the historic environment*, (PPG-15, DoE and DNH, 1994).

> There is a growing appreciation not just of the architectural set-pieces, but of many more structures, especially industrial, agricultural, and other vernacular buildings that, although sometimes individually unassuming, collectively reflect some of the most distinctive and creative aspects of English history. More than this, our understanding and appreciation of the historic environment now stretches beyond buildings to the spaces and semi-natural features which people have also moulded, and which are often inseparable from the buildings themselves. For example, the pattern of roads and open spaces and the views they create within historic townscapes may be as valuable as the buildings. In the countryside, the detailed patterns of fields and farms, of hedgerows and walls, and of hamlets and villages, are among the most highly valued aspects of our environment.
>
> PPG-15, para 6.2:

It is English Heritage's view that the best interests of the historic landscape, or its future sensible conservation, would not be well served by rigorous protection through inflexible constraints of a small sample of the whole. On the basis of this position, government has also advised planning authorities that:

> Appraisals based on assessment of the historic character of the whole countryside will be more flexible, and more likely to be effectively integrated

Fig 3: Changing landscape: post-medieval intakes reverting to upland vegetation in the Forest of Bowland, North Lancashire

> with the aims of the planning process, than an attempt to define selected areas for additional control. It is unlikely therefore to be feasible to prepare a definitive register at a national level of England's wider historic landscape. The whole of the landscape, to varying degrees and in different ways, is an archaeological and historic artefact, the product of complex historic processes and past land use. It is also a crucial and defining aspect of biodiversity (and much of its value lies in its complexity, regional diversity and local distinctiveness, qualities which a national register cannot adequately define.
>
> PPG-15, para 6.40

The 1991 policy statement also set out four basic principles. These were at that stage framed in the context of the debate about a possible register, but they are equally applicable to improved understanding or assessment of the historic landscape at any level. As ways of influencing future landscape change and of achieving its managed evolution, they are also relevant to both the planning process and to land management regimes.

These principles, the basic objectives for EH's historic landscape strategy, contained four requirements:

- all historical elements of the landscape must be included, and not just those individual features traditionally classified as historic buildings or ancient monuments

- methods are required to enable some comparison of the different historic interest or character of different areas of landscape, in order to aid planning and resource allocation; this is not necessarily the same as evaluation as it has been conventionally practised

- a methodology is required for characterising the historic dimension of the countryside which could be used equally by landowners or local authorities and other government departments or agencies, as well as by English Heritage, for the national or local identification, understanding, and grading of historic landscape

- the method must be able to inform and assist local management conservation decisions at all levels, from the strategic and national to the day-to-day work of landowners and others who live on the land

The parallel consultation paper, which was issued towards the end of 1991 (English Heritage 1991d), sought views from a wide range of archaeologists, conservationists, landscape practitioners, and planners, as well as from landowning and other countryside interests, on five broad topics:

- the scope of the term 'historic environment' or 'historic landscape'

- the need for landscape to be allowed to continue to change

- appropriate methodologies for identification of the historic landscape

- the practicality of evaluating relative importance of components

- the need and desirability for any new specialised designation

Responses, while wide-ranging in detail, were very largely supportive of the main ideas, notably the desirability of a broad definition and extensive scope for the term 'historic landscape', and the idea that landscape conservation should be holistic in its approach. There was significant support for some level of national consistency in methods of assessing or evaluating historic landscape, although both the idea of grading and the possibility of a new formal register were not received well by all consultees, many of whom felt that existing measures in the planning system already have the potential to offer an appropriate balance.

Recent developments in ideas on landscape

The 1990 White Paper did not mark the beginning of English Heritage's concerns with the historic landscape, because its statutory remit has always been drawn very widely (English Heritage 1990). The organisation's principal focus has more often been on individual ancient monuments or historic buildings, but the setting of historic buildings, for example, has always been an important concern, and since 1986 we have been compiling a register of historic parks and gardens, which affords protection through the planning system to the designed component of the landscape (English Heritage 1991a and 1991c). We have also worked hard to ensure that the settings of ancient monuments are not neglected by the planning process. In urban areas, and occasionally in rural areas too, long-standing work with local authorities on the preservation and enhancement of Conservation Areas has led to an area-based, rather than a site-based perspective. In the countryside more widely (MAFF and English Heritage 1992), the publication of *Ancient monuments in the countryside* (Darvill 1987) was a first step towards connecting the survival and management of individual archaeologi-

Fig 4: Post-medieval and later fields on ex-downland in Hampshire

cal sites with their wider landscape context, using the framework of broadly defined habitats and land use types, such as wetlands, arable land, pasture, or woodland (Macinnes and Wickham-Jones 1992).

The move from appreciating and preserving individual sites to an understanding of the need to protect and conserve their settings as well, was perhaps the most important initial stimulus for developing our concern for the wider historic landscape. The concept is not new; it has been part of planning policy, at least for ancient monuments, since 1973 (DoE Planning Circular 22/73). The concept of curtilage in conservation has been in existence since the inception of listed building control, but as English Heritage's statu-

statutory responsibility and powers largely centre on sites, the protection of setting has been less central to its work. Since 1981, however, the stronger controls on scheduled monuments introduced by the 1979 Act have enabled resource managers to pay more attention to the surroundings and contexts of archaeological sites through the planning system. As the concept of setting became more established, the more obvious it became that the wider historic landscape was still largely unconsidered; this growing perception was one of the seeds of the concern expressed in the DoE's 1990 white paper leading later to publication of *Sustainable Development: the UK strategy* (DoE 1994b).

A parallel widening of perception came through the 1970s and 1980s as archaeology, and archaeological research broadened its scope. There were several dimensions to this: the growth of landscape archaeology, taking as its study the past at landscape scale, and the related acceptance that archaeological sites can be very extensive, covering many square kilometres (eg the Dartmoor Reave sytems, Gerrard 1998). There was also, more simply, an explosion in the density and geographical spread of archaeological data resulting from increasingly properly resourced rescue work from the mid-1970s onwards. Finally, there was the contribution of 'new' archaeological theories, which encouraged recognition of the importance of space as well as time, of the idea that the spaces 'between' sites can be as important and tell us as much about the past as the sites themselves, and, indeed, of non-site-based theoretical archaeology as a whole. All these trends necessitated, at some stage, a more considered approach to historic landscape within conservation theory (Macinnes 1994).

English Heritage has reflected all these changes in recent years in various ways, by:

- using the *Register of Parks and Gardens of Special Historic Interest in England*, and some extensive scheduling, to push site-level designation procedures to their limits. This has also demonstrated that the combination of large areas and 'living' historic sites requires an approach radically different to site-based systems, in the sense that without management of land cover and of semi-natural features the parkland or gardens will lose their value

- devising a simple categorisation of the building blocks of the historic landscape (such as archaeological sites, hedges and boundry walls, structures, and semi-natural features), not because we believe that the landscape could or should be reduced to its parts, but because examination of components as a part of interpretation and analysis is a valid step towards understanding the mechanisms which have created historic landscape character

- demonstrating that, if required, it is possible to use selected components to score individual areas to produce comparative estimates of importance and value; the early pilot project that English Heritage commissioned in Kent set out a method of doing this (*summarised in annex 1*). It is a system that may have future uses, preferably so that like can be compared with like, within a rigorously defined region such as those defined by the Countryside character map (English Nature 1998; Countryside Commission forthcoming b), or the MPP's *An atlas of rural settlement in England* (Roberts and Wrathmell forthcoming)

- experimenting with the use of expert judgement to define the most important areas of historic landscape, an approach sometimes labelled 'top-down'; two of the projects reported on here (Oxfordshire and Durham, *see chapters 7 and 8*) tested such an approach. It clearly has some value, but it is most effective when underpinned or guided by a clear framework derived from data-led work. English Heritage does not believe that by itself it offers a defensible method of identifying historic landscape for protection or management

Fig 5: Lead-mining affected landscape in the White Peak, Derbyshire

English Heritage's current view

Historic landscape studies have regularly been side-tracked by discussions about definition. It is wise to avoid too much concern with precise definition, for, in truth, many terms and many 'languages' can be used to express the indivisibility and cultural or historic dimension of the land-

indivisibility and cultural or historic dimension of the landscape, from the simple claim that 'everything connects', to more complicated space-driven or holistic constructs. One current approach, useful because it commands the attention and perhaps the resources of government and other policy-makers, is through the rhetoric of biodiversity and sustainability. These terms recognise that the countryside is an environmental whole, and that it is the sum of all its parts. They recognise, too, that the countryside is vulnerable, that its survival depends on careful demand management, and that land-use planning should be informed by a combined approach to value, understanding, and appreciation. The idea of biodiversity, in particular, accepts that landscape is a human habitat as much as it is a natural habitat (Fairclough 1994a). It is people, in the past and still today, who are the prime creators and regulators of biodiversity.

Any practical approach to landscape character must steer firmly away from using sites and other types of point-data as the basis for understanding. More broadly based methods are needed which can relate to extensive areas and most of all to interrelationships and interactions. Within this approach, overall characterisation of the historic dimension of the landscape will provide a framework for conservation decisions. This is the core of the argument presented here as the results of the *Historic Landscape Project*. It meets our need to take account of the historic dimension of the whole countryside, and produces assessments which vary in detail from area to area, but do not leave 'white areas' that appear to be judged as having no value whatsoever in historic terms. This is not to say that all areas are nationally important, but is rather to empower local communities, land managers, planning authorities, and national agencies such as ourselves, to take sensible decisions, based on good understanding of the past, about the future of the landscape.

It is also the case, because the historic landscape embraces semi-natural as well as archaeological features, and is the product as much of present-day perceptions as of historical truth, that landscape conservation cannot be achieved by archaeologists alone. Both its study and its management should be genuinely multi-disciplinary. In the institutional framework of national conservation agencies this means closer integration of the concerns of English Heritage with those of bodies working for nature conservation and the protection of the landscape more generally. English Heritage has already, for several years, been successfully working more closely with English Nature and the Countryside Commission to achieve joint and mutually supportive programmes (Fairclough 1995).

The successful implementation of such a strategy will require multiple instruments, not simply designations, but a more balanced combination of existing instruments such as the planning system, the agri-environmental programme, the reformed Conservation Area Partnership schemes, and local countryside management strategies and farm plans. Partnerships need to extend beyond government bodies (MAFF, DoE) to local communities and landowners.

Although mentioned last, local community involvement ought to be given high priority. The English landscape is particularly notable for its great regional diversity, and even more so for its local character. Relatively insignificant features (the individual methods of construction of a field wall, a local style of field gateway, architectural styles and materials of humble houses and farm buildings, the presence of minor archaeological sites) may not of themselves be of national importance, but come into their own at the scale of landscape character because they contribute to what makes one landscape different to another. In this way, local character can be an issue of national importance (English Heritage 1997a, 1997b).

Historic landscape character cannot, however, at least in the first instance, be assessed or appreciated at local level, no matter how significant the contribution it makes to a local character. A broader view, embracing both a national overview and a regional-level assessment, is needed to allow the overall pattern to be appreciated and to give context to individual features. At the national level, we have the MPP *Settlement mapping project* and the incorporation of cultural factors into the *Countryside character map*. At regional level, the example provided by the historic landscape characterisation study of Cornwall (*see annex 2*) is being followed elsewhere, (*see chapter 11*) and within Cornwall is proving to be a useful management and planning tool. All of this work is founded on the general principles established by the *Historic Landscape Project* described here.

2: The countryside context

Graham Fairclough

All the areas of work outlined in chapter 1 formed antecedents for the *Historic Landscape Project*. Of additional importance to the inception of the project, however, was the work of the other national government agencies concerned with managing the environment.

English Heritage's concern with the historic landscape is shared very strongly by the Countryside Commission (now Agency), which exists to promote the conservation and enjoyment of the countryside, and whose work rests very largely upon an appreciation of the character and quality of landscape. Landscape character, and methods of assessing it, have been the subject of much Countryside Commission guidance (Countryside Commission 1993).

The Commission's view of landscape is holistic. The belief that landscape is the sum of all its parts, and that landscape character is a reflection of history and archaeology as well as of its scenic and visual values or its ecology, is well established in Countryside Commission thinking and it underpins the definition of 'natural beauty' used for the definition and management of National Parks and Areas of Outstanding Natural Beauty (AONBs) (Lloyd 1994).

The Commission is also fully wedded to the concept of active conservation and of integration (Countryside Commission *et al* 1993; English Heritage *et al* 1996). The present landscape has reached its existing forms predominantly as a result of human interaction with nature, principally by means of traditional long-term management practices. Without the continuation of this management landscape character will change and be modified, by ecological interventions, if not by human activities. It therefore can neither be fixed nor left untouched as a museum or reserve.

At one level, landscape changes could be welcomed as merely further evidence of the continuing evolution of a long-changed landscape: the latest overlay to the palimpsest, or a further contribution to time-depth, although conscious decisions could also be taken that some changes (or some directions of change) are more desirable than others, ie 'managed evolution'. This requires understanding of the forms that the landscape has taken as it has come down to us, that is of the many and varied processes that have shaped it. To achieve well managed evolution, traditional practices will in some instances need to be maintained (as at Laxton, the famous surviving, collectively farmed open field system in Nottinghamshire). Where past practices are lost beyond recall it is necessary either to find alternative practices, in order to produce a similar effect or to help the creation of a new landscape, which will keep whatever is necessary from the past, but also add to it in ways that prolong, or are in sympathy with, past directions.

This concern with helping to shape the future landscape lies at the root of the need for archaeological conservation to integrate with landscape conservation. Landscape conservation, and notably the techniques of landscape

Fig 6: Landscape patterns industry and territorial divisions in the Lune Valley at Quernmore, North Lancashire

assessment which the Countryside Commission has developed and promoted, is also one of the most promising opportunities for enlarging and disseminating an archaeological appreciation of the historic and archaeological dimensions of the landscape. English Heritage has for long accepted, and promoted, the view, that information is a prerequisite for the conservation of archaeology and buildings (English Heritage 1992), and that the principle is similar for the whole landscape, where 'information' will usually be in the form of landscape characterisation. This view is enshrined in *Planning policy guidance note 16: archaeology and planning* (PPG-16) (DoE 1990b) and PPG-15 (DoE/DNH 1994).

In parallel with the English Heritage project, therefore, and with English Heritage assistance, the Countryside Commission has also expanded its own concepts and methods for understanding the historic landscape. A consultation document was published in 1994 (Countryside Commission 1994a), which was subsequently reissued in a definitive form in 1996.

The Countryside Commission also explored ways of recognising the historic dimension of the landscape in the south-west England pilot for *A new map of England* (Countryside Commission 1994b), and the results of this early work informed the development of the national Countryside Character Project. As a result, using new research commissioned jointly by the Countryside Commission and English Heritage, the *Countryside character map* was prepared on the basis of twelve variables, of which five related to specific historic or archaeological aspects of landscape character. These 'cultural variables' included, for example, the visual contribution of archaeological sites to the landscape, the regional pattern of settlement types, field system diversity and form, and industrial archaeology. The regional character areas have therefore grown out of the historic as much as the scenic or ecological dimension of the landscape, and the published character area descriptions demonstrate this (Countryside Commission 1998, and Agency 1999). Equally important, when more detailed description is carried out, techniques of historic landscape assessment will be able to focus in more detail on the archaeology of the landscape within these compatible and homogeneous zones.

Over the same period, English Heritage has developed closer working links with English Nature. English Nature has taken a similar course to English Heritage in moving away from purely site-based conservation towards an area or landscape-based framework. In doing so, it has taken on the concept of culturally determined biodiversity, recognising that the present pattern of English flora and fauna has been heavily modified

Fig 7: Lanercost, Cumbria, aerial view (photo: English Heritage/Skyscan).

by human activity: ie that biodiversity and historic landscape are unchanging concepts. Its *Natural Areas*, a set of sub-regional areas characterised in biogeographical terms, but compatible with the Countryside Commission's (1996) *Countryside Character Areas*, is intended to provide a national strategic policy framework for most of its work, and to be the basis for landscape-scale conservation into the next century (English Nature 1998).

Each *Natural Area* possesses a distinctive mix of habitat and ecology, many closely determined by geology and topography. Many are recognisably historic zones as well, which is a further illustration of the cultural underpinning to biodiversity. Each *Natural Area* can be characterised by broadly defined 'cultural affinities' which distinguish it from other *Natural Areas*: the ancient enclosed fields and managed woodlands of the Chilterns, for example, and the distinctive prehistoric and medieval landscape systems of Bodmin or Dartmoor; or the intensive agricultural use of the Northumberland coastal plain, with its legacy of Improvement Age field systems and model farmsteads preserving fragmentary survivals of earlier landscape. The history of the area's ecology is a major component of the *Natural Area Profiles*, descriptions of which English Nature has published (English Nature 1998).

Definition of these cultural affinities throughout the country would be a fruitful task, providing a way of measuring at regional scale the coincidence and interrelationship of archaeology and ecology. It could also further our appreciation of archaeology's regional diversity, and provide a framework for more detailed local study and analysis, whether of archaeological sites and patterning or of historic landscape (as a set of study areas, and perhaps a set of preliminary research agendas).

The *Natural Areas* and the *Countryside Character Project* mirror the growing concern of archaeologists for landscape-scale study and conservation. All represent the same evolution of thought. The widening of archaeological interest from monuments (or sites) to their setting and context, and thence to the wider interrelated system which we term *Historic Landscape*, is reflected in nature conservation's move from species protection, to habitat conservation, and now to a concern for the whole countryside and to landscape ecology (Selman 1994). Both disciplines recognise that protection of small 'reserves' is often uneconomic and philosophically flawed, and is in the longer term unsustainable. A greater concern for the whole landscape, even in a broad-brush way, is likely to facilitate site protection (for example encouraging sympathetic land use on a regional basis or on a whole farm eg *Environmentally Sensitive Areas* (ESAs).

This approach is supported at Government level by the *UK Action plan for biodiversity* (DoE 1994a), especially the recognition of the importance of habitats rather than of individual species. The *Biodiversity action plan* also recognises the central role of past human activity in creating, modifying, or enhancing biodiversity and the landscape settings that nurture it. There are therefore highly important links between historic landscape (the remains of the past interaction between people and their environment) and modern habitats and biodiversity. For some, the term 'cultural landscape' summarises this relationship.

The landscape projects of the three countryside agencies – English Nature's *Natural Areas*, the Countryside Commission's *Countryside Character Project*, and English Heritage's *Historic Landscape Project*, the last of which is reported here – have thus been running on convergent tracks. This convergence is deliberate, and will give the foundation for integrated longer-term strategies for countryside conservation into the next century, whether for research, for agricultural policy, or for development planning. We hope, too, that it will strongly inform government rural and agri-environmental policy.

Guiding principles

The approach developed during the *Historic Landscape Project*, and which we are advocating here and through a series of county-wide characterisation projects, takes into account a series of key principles which should underlie historic landscape conservation. These include:

- the landscape is a historic artefact which everywhere in England is culturally shaped

- its evolution has been complex, passing through change and continuity, and its present appearance reflects thousands of years of historic processes, human decisions, and changes in land use

- it is the product of dynamic and change, and for the future there is the inevitability of further change: landscape conservation is about managing future evolution, not about preventing change

- change and evolution will create new or modified landscape; there can be no question of attempting to return to past landscape by any process of reconstruction

- it would in any event be undesirable to prevent change. The landscape is a living artefact: the withdrawal of appropriate management, by allowing natural succession to change long-established patterns of land use and land cover (such as the encroachment of heather onto upland intakes in the Cumbrian Lake District) can be as damaging in its own timescale as golf course or motorway construction. Change, when properly planned, will usually be more acceptable than fossilisation

Fig 8: Hadrian's wall: Birdoswald Fort, Cumbria, aerial view (Photo, English Heritage/Skyscan)

These principles are now widely accepted. They underpin most approaches to sustainability, such as that set out in *Sustaining the historic environment* (English Heritage 1997a). They have also been carried to a wider European audience, through the general principle outlined in the Helsinki Declaration (Council of Europe 1996). They also directly underpin the philosophy of the Council of Europe's draft *European landscape convention* (CLRAE 1998)

3: Philosophy and interpretation

Graham Fairclough

Consideration of historic landscape issues is far from being a 'new' topic, and there have been too many sterile and inconclusive debates on definition. Archaeology, for example, has been engaged in a variety of ways in the development of 'landscape archaeology' since the 1970s at least, while historical geographers' concern for the landscape is of an even longer pedigree, notably in the study of field systems and enclosures. There is thus a large literature on historic landscape and related subjects. (eg Cosgrove 1990, Brandon and Millman 1978, Goodchild 1990, Hoskins 1955, Landscape Research Group 1988, and Swanwick 1989)

In historic or archaeological disciplines, the study of the designed aspect of the landscape is also well developed, with the consequence that for many people the words *'historic landscape'* appear to be synonymous with parks and gardens, to the exclusion of the remainder of the landscape. Before describing the work of the English Heritage project, therefore, it is necessary, while avoiding narrow arguments about definition, to take stock of what is meant here by the words 'historic landscape'.

The full chronological sweep of historic landscape formation in England (for at least the past 5000 years, and probably much longer, although any lasting physical landscape impact of human activity is perhaps arguable for the Mesolithic period), and the complete breadth of the social, economic, and political systems and processes represented, can best, perhaps only, be explored through archaeology.

The English landscape is nowhere completely natural: even fields or moorland can be shown to display the changing force of human action, whether through ancient soil impoverishment or the creation of new soils, or through more recent industrial activity; and there are very few areas that are now not in sight of some type of built structure, whether isolated farmhouse or field wall. (MAFF and English Heritage 1992) Only the underlying geology may be unchanged, but this itself has not always been the overriding determinant on human manufacture of landscape that it is sometimes taken to be. Its influence has often been overridden by cultural imperatives. The landscape is primarily an artefact, a human product (Fairclough 1994a; Countryside Commission 1994a, 1991). Its evolution is visible to us in its material remains, and archaeology is the proper discipline for the study of its historical dimension. (*see also* Larsen 1992 and Wägenbaum 1993)

Fig 9: Chalk downland and enclosure, North Wiltshire

Archaeological methods can bring us to the heart of landscape history (those social processes which have created chronologically specific land use and territorially based activities that have shaped the landscape), but landscape is also an artefact in the further sense. It is landscape, whether viewed in historic terms or not, and particularly when seen as an ideational construct or the product of perception, that can be said at one level to exist only when thought, seen, or experienced (eg Shanks 1993, 141 3). In other words landscape is culturally determined in two ways: because it is the product of human, ie cultural, decisions about land use, and because it is understood through a set of perceptions which are themselves culturally and historically conditioned.

At the same time, the landscape has shaped past societies. It has been used to pass on rules for land use and for social behaviour and religious belief from one generation to the next. This intergenerational role of the landscape, especially, but not exclusively, in preliterate societies, ought not to be underestimated. Our landscape in this sense is far from being 'natural', but has been organised in a variety of ways in order to guide land-use decisions, register ownership and create group identity (Fairclough 1994a, 68).

Past society can be studied through its material remains at object or site level, and landscape-led analysis can generate an understanding of the political and social fabric of a society, the economic relationships between people, the social negotiation of space and privilege, and the allocation and division of power. Social or functional activities do not take place in isolation from their environment, but are not shaped exclusively by it (cf Graves 1994, 160). The 'grammar' of the landscape created by one generation has been an important vehicle for guiding the way it has been used by its descendants.

Space (ie the spatial structures for living which people have created), whether at building or landscape scale (Fairclough 1992, 1999a), is simultaneously both a product of, and a framework for, social behaviour. Environmental and geographical determinants will have some part to play in this analysis, but our knowledge of human capacity to change and control the landscape, even in the Neolithic period, should warn us of the need not to overestimate environmental influences. Having said that, some human actions in the past have created new environmental constraints (just as they threaten to in the future) and it is a mistake to assume that past cultural systems have always been sustainable and in harmony with their environment, and that only landscapes that demonstrate such 'harmony' are important.

Much of this ground has been considered in the *Historic Landscape Project* and reported here. The aim was to develop a clear framework tailored to our need to facilitate and promote landscape conservation. The following section introduces in outline a few of the key principles and ideas which guided the project, and underpin the work described in the remainder of this book.

Indivisibility

It was decided at an early stage to use the term 'historic landscape' to denote the potential of almost any tract of land in England (howsoever defined topographically) to be read, or interpreted, as a record of its own history and evolution at the hands of successive generations of farmers, industrialists, and others over several thousand years. The term is deliberately and consciously used in the singular as a collective noun because it does not denote any particular area, and it carries no connotation that any one area is 'an historic landscape' where other areas are not. Indeed, the English Heritage view is that 'historic landscapes' do not exist as definable entities, and that it would be erroneous and ineffective to attempt to transfer techniques suited to the classification or designation of specific discrete and bounded sites to the different requirements of landscape conservation. Historic landscape must be considered an integral whole; it cannot sensibly be deconstructed into a set of discrete sites without loss of understanding of its significant character. Instead, the terms *historic landscape character*, or *character of the historic landscape* (with *historic landscape* as useful shorthand) are used throughout this book.

Integration and the overlapping of social values

An even wider aspect to landscape is that the concept of the indivisibility of the *historic landscape* (ie that there are no unhistoric portions of the landscape) is central to any debate on integrated management. Whether it is described as historic or not, the wider view that landscape simultaneously demands and offers can encourage an holistic approach. Landscape is the sum of all its parts (Fairclough 1995). Its ecological aspects are already being mapped and characterised as carefully as its scenic and visual attributes have been for several years (Countryside Commission 1993), and there are the beginnings of a similar concern to understand the historical dimension of the landscape just as thoroughly (Countryside Commission 1994a, 1994e, 1996).

Fig 10: Kenilworth Castle, Warwickshire, aerial view (Photo: English Heritage/Skyscan)

In social terms, the landscape is valued by many sections of the community for a variety of reasons, not-necessarily mutually exclusive: for its fauna and flora, or for its broader natural attributes; because it is seen to be aesthetically satisfying, or to carry artistic, literary, or other cultural associations; or because it is the site for leisure and recreation in 'different' surroundings; all as well as for its archaeological or historical meaning (English Heritage 1997a). Historic landscape also has many levels, from the national vista of work such as the Countryside Commission's new mapping project, the *Countryside Character Programme* (Countryside Commission 1994b, forthcoming b) or the MPP's mapping and classification work (eg of settlement type and pattern) (Roberts and Wrathmell 1995, forthcoming), to the regional and local scales of, for example, county landscape assessments or farm survey grants.

Landscape as human artefact

The term *historic landscape* should also be seen as a metaphor which refers to the concept that the whole landscape is made by human activity. It carries with it the idea that landscape is the physical manifestation of the interaction of people and the environment through time. It is also, however, a forum, or context for modern-day discourse, to bring together otherwise separate, perhaps conflicting, environmental, conservation, and socio-economic concerns. It is therefore, as a concept, one of the best vehicles for integrating the different aspects of conservation: for entering into dialogue with landowners and farmers, for making connections to the principles of sustainability (state of environment reports via landscape assessments) and biodiversity (its history and causes), or for establishing frameworks to take account of both natural and historic values. It can also help to encourage public awareness, and public accessibility to the landscape (on all levels, but recently, physical access).

Environmental capital

Finally, and this has particular reference to archaeology and nature conservation, the concept that all landscape is 'historic' can help us to avoid the constraints and limitations of selective protection by designation, which might protect sites selected as displaying aspects of importance while allowing the quality of the landscape as a whole to be eroded to the point where the individually protected sites within it have their value reduced. It has recently been suggested, for example, that national policy has, more or less successfully, protected rare bird species but that now the relatively common species are at risk through wholesale reduction of once common and widespread habitats.

There are obvious archaeological parallels: deserted villages preserved without the context of the remains of their contemporary fields; barrows as islands preserved in inappropriate settings. At the same time, the concept that the historic character of all areas needs to be considered enables planners and others to give due weight to regional diversity and to local character and distinctiveness, as well as to national importance.

More significantly, this approach to historic landscape character will also provide an essential major component for the establishment of criteria for the assessment of sustainable development. The early division of environmental resources into the general baseline of the resource (constant capital) and its more selective key highlights (its critical assets) (English Heritage *et al* 1993,

10–11) was too crude, but has since been refined with greater emphasis on the idea of 'capital' rather than its subdivisions (English Heritage 1997a; Countryside Commission *et al* 1997). Any approach to the characterisation of the resource, however, is most readily adapted to the needs of archaeology and the historic environment if constant capital is defined, assessed, and evaluated at landscape scale. Key highlights of the resource can be identified fairly straightforwardly (eg Darvill *et al* 1987, in the context of the Monuments Protection Programme) , but point or site-based information is less likely to be relevant to attempts to assess the significant character of the cultural parts of the environmental resources.

Complexity and variety

The results of the *Historic Landscape Project* (*see Part II*) also underline the need to avoid any simplified view of historic landscapes as definable topographic entities. Attempts to create and adopt a system of landscape classification (eg 'enclosure landscape', 'ancient landscape', 'industrial landscape', and even less logically or sustainably, relict landscape') prove neither practical nor sustainable in terms of the decisions needed for the management of the historic landscape, however useful they may be as tools for understanding specific episodes of landscape history.

It was a basic precept of the project that just as the landscape is everywhere historic in one way or another, so it is that any area will display several aspects of its past, or several attributes of historic character. These will overlap with each other and between areas, and it is an unhelpful oversimplification to list areas in terms of any one of these attributes, no matter how predominant. The trajectory of any area's landscape evolution is also likely to be distinctive, and it has proved impractical to define 'types' of historic landscape from which a selection for protection, for example, could be made. This has been a successful approach for monuments and buildings, which are discrete entities, but the *Historic Landscape Project* recognised from the outset that this essentially site-based approach should not be transferred to landscape. Any area of landscape will have a long evolution, and many successive episodes or chronological horizons are likely to leave their mark in it. There are very few simple, single-phase landscapes in England. Almost all are both multi-period and multi-functional.

In the work reported in this book, therefore, precedence was given to 'time-depth' (to the

Fig 11: Lead-mining affected landscape and post-medieval enclosure in the White Peak, Derbyshire

archaeological/historic succession, in terms borrowed from ecology), to the palimpsest of the landscape, and to local and regional variety/character (with obvious debts to Common Ground's work) rather than to academic typology and classification.

Process and dynamics

While its main study is of the surviving physical remains of the past within the landscape, the aim of historic landscape conservation is broader. It is to understand the processes and mechanism which lie behind the formation of, changes to, and survival of historic landscape remains (Countryside Commission 1994a, 1994e, 1996). Conservation is not concerned merely to survey material remains in isolation from the events that created and re-formed them, any more than they should be preserved in isolation from each other. These cultural causes or processes might be social, religious, economic, or political, or most probably a combination of all of these. The causes can be defined using any one of the current archaeological paradigms, but basic to the use of the term is the attempt to understand the current landscape and its development as well as to describe and characterise it.

While emphasising historical depth and causality, however, the project did not ignore the role and importance of current, modern perception, whether this be in aesthetic, associative, or amenity terms. Given however that English Heritage and the Countryside Commission both have important roles within historic landscape conservation, the main weight of interest in modern-day social and personal perceptions lies with the Countryside Commission, while English Heritage takes the lead on the contribution of non-visible archaeology (eg burial sites, crop marks) or historical causation lacking material remains to historic landscape character.

Patterns and interrelationships

Within historic landscape study, individual sites or features are important, not for themselves but for their contribution to a larger landscape pattern. Key concepts here, as in Wales, where the Countryside Commission for Wales is developing them in practical terms (Kelly 1994, Cadw 1998), are the ideas of components (eg settlement sites, buildings, hedges) and systems (at local level settlement and field patterns, and also at regional intraterritorial level), of coherence (the extent to which historically-identifiable systems are still visible and understandable in the landscape), and of articulation (the extent to which features in a system are still related one to the other). All these ideas can be measured using criteria such as survival, completeness, rarity, or representivity. Their use does not mean that the landscape is being reduced to its components, although it is important to guard against reductionism: the integrity of the whole (which at times might involve regional or national perspectives) must be kept firmly in view.

Scales

It is possible to take account of historic landscape at several scales, using spatial concepts and ideas of patterns and interrelationship (Fairclough 1999a). This enables questions such as change and continuity, the ways in which they are combined through time, and the role of historic processes and causation to be considered. It also highlights, particularly perhaps at regional scale, the way in which 'historic landscape' depends significantly on current perception. It is essential throughout to keep in mind the inherent complexity of the landscape and its origins, and the diversity of ways in which its development can now be read in the landscape.

Three attributes: site articulation; territorial interrelationship; and regional pattern may be regarded as occupying a scale from the local to the regional, or in archaeological terms from site and feature, through system and territory, to regional diversity (see, for example, Darvill *et al* 1993). On this scale, assessment or judgement will be based at site level largely on data, at the middle level on archaeological models, and towards the regional patterning end of the scale increasing emphasis will be laid in most cases on broader perceptions.

Site articulation expresses the ways in which individual features or components of the landscape cohere to create landscape-scale complexes, both in past and present-day landscapes (while taking into account ideas such as palimpsest and time-depth as well as space). Succession and change need to be considered, in order to demonstrate the ways in which one generation's landscape, though historically and culturally specific in itself, was always fitted within an inherited framework.

A broad view should be taken of the range of features which contribute, through this local articulation, to the overall landscape. Conventional archaeological sites are most obvious, but palaeo-environmental deposits of all kinds have an explanatory role. Local patterns of historic land cover (the reservation of land for common grazing, or the creation of spiritual space) is often both one of the articulated elements and also the matrix within which that articulation can be read. The principal framework will usually be the land and field divisions of hedge, bank, or wall, the interconnections of road and track, and the scale of settlement and farmstead hierarchy. Some landscape components contribute to site-level articulation in a more limited way (eg major strategic land-use decisions; moor and heath transhumance, the

upper levels of settlement hierarchy) but come to the fore at the mid-scale (territorial) level of interrelationships between systems.

Territorial interrelationships through a more abstracted level of archaeological interpretation, offer understanding of the way that local landscape systems, ie locally-articulated sites, interlock at a more regional level. These are the relationships which demonstrate, for example, the long-distance symbiosis of urban centres, or of the connection between sites such as long barrows or henges and their catchment areas and hinterlands, or of satellite farmsteads around hillforts, or villa estates around Roman cities, or the sophisticated market hierarchy of, say, London and East Anglia in the late middle ages. Attempts by today's planners to understand what sustainable development means for the industrialised urban world may also come to fall into this category. It also, however, enables other land-use relationships to be explored, such as the common use of distant upland areas by lowland farming communities, mirroring, on a regional scale, a parish or township's reservation of common resources for wood and grazing at the parish edge. The dissolution of these long-distance ties can also create historically-specific landscapes, when dependencies adapt from being specialised grazing areas to being self-supporting independent townships.

Regional patterning finally is a term that attempts to summarise a way of reading meaning into regional diversity. It need not exclude considerations of local character, but its main focus is to demonstrate broad patterns over large tracts of land. These patterns can be read in past landscape, but they are more valuable for English Heritage's purposes when considered again the backdrop of the present-day landscape. This allows the patterning of landscape to reflect survival and condition, which are of course conditioned by historical factors. It also connects with ways of valuing and using the landscape that are not primarily archaeological, such as visual and scenic assessment, emotional and artistic attachment and concern for the natural world. Even these, however, are also historically-conditioned values.

Attributes

An alternative threefold approach, less closely correlated to scale and more applicable at any level of resolution, is to approach historic landscape via three of the attributes which characterise, at least in England, the landscape's historical basis. These attributes are less straightforward to categorise, but they are perhaps closer to an historical understanding of the landscape. These are historical process, time-depth, and complexity with diversity.

Historical process concerns explanation and causation. Processes might include the effect of social factors (such as modes of inheritance) as well as more functional processes related directly to agriculture (such as early prehistoric clearance or the subsequent long-term grazing of upland areas) or to industry and more ideological aspects (such as landscape formation used to validate power and social hierarchy).

Time-depth brings greater appreciation of the chronological combinations of change and continuity which create the historic landscape, and focuses rather more on description.

Complexity and diversity is necessarily at a descriptive and analytical level, in order to identify historic landscape character or to characterise an area's historic dimension and origins. Complexity is perhaps the one aspect of historic landscape that is most significant, and which ought not to be underestimated.

Transparency and the myth of relict landscape

The visibility of landscape is a separate issue which needs mentioning briefly here. The broad definition of landscape, as adopted by English Heritage, centres on the physical remains of landscape

succession existing within the present landscape. It does not rule out the possibility and value of studying and reconstructing past landscape horizons, but it does, however, leave no room for the concept of 'relict landscape'. This idea is flawed even when used to try to define a separate, identifiable, class or type of landscape. In terms of present landscape character, however, it is an even less meaningful construct. It could logically be taken to mean relict horizons (ie past layers within the present landscape's time-depth), or there could be a logical use of the term as in 'relict component' (as for example disused field walls or lynchets underlying later, still-used, fields).

The term 'relict' cannot however properly be applied to the whole of a landscape or even to an area of landscape of any size. Landscape in itself is never relict. The south-west uplands of Dartmoor or of Bodmin, far from being the 'relict prehistoric landscape' of recent archaeological myth, are complex developed landscapes which have passed through three or four main episodes in time (early agriculture, late prehistoric animal grazing or sacred space; temporary medieval resettlement in the climactic/demographic optimum; and recent widespread reclamation and enclosure). All of these stages (agriculture, religion, politics, and industry) can still generally be read in the landscape, and remnants of all these episodes, themes, and functions are still frequently visible at landscape scale. Yet the landscape is still a late-twentieth-century one, perceived and experienced, and most importantly worked and managed, in the present.

In a similar way, the large scale seventeenth to eighteenth century AD enclosure landscape of eastern England retains elements of earlier, quite different, ways of farming the land collectively, just as elsewhere (eg Northumberland) medieval

Fig 12: Peveril Castle, Derbyshire, panorama, (photo: English Heritage/Skyscan)

hamlets with fields were succeeded by large free-standing farmsteads in the period of rationalisation in the eighteenth to nineteenth centuries. Other landscape areas demonstrate long-standing continuity, such as the anciently-enclosed and long-settled areas known from at least the 1st millennium BC in Cornwall or East Anglia. This is a fundamental continuity, however, and much change of detail, of land use, settlement and building style, has skated over its surface; this too is legible in today's countryside.

Dartmoor, one of the areas most frequently described as a relict landscape, is in fact a post-medieval pastoral landscape of rough grazing within which earlier features, notably the reaves systems or tin-mining, are visible. Northamptonshire's ridge and furrow is equally a 'relict' feature within later enclosed landscape but is not itself a 'relict landscape'. To claim that it is ignores, or understates, both earlier and later horizons, as well as other less visible components of the contemporary environment which can also easily be overlooked. This is partly a matter of scale, relationship, and context, and partly one of transparency (some historic land uses facilitate the appreciation of the remains of previous uses, others conceal or destroy time-depth). It also reveals again the dichotomy between monument-based and landscape-based systems of interpretation. These distinctions underlie the conclusions of the *Historic Landscape Project* reported in Part II.

The integrity of the present landscape

All landscape is both of the present and in a continuing state of development. The complex

Fig 13: Post-medieval enclosure of earlier open field and upland pasture at Edlingham, Northumberland

relationship between past and present should not be unduly simplified. In particular the dichotomy of continuity and discontinuity can be over-simplified. Visibility of earlier episodes of landscape history is not the only measure of significance. For this reason the English Heritage project did not use the distinction between 'relict' and 'continuing landscape' which is embedded in current UNESCO *World Heritage Site guidelines for the landscape* (ICOMOS UK1994a).

In contrast, and in close alignment to emerging European concepts for the cultural landscape, English Heritage considers that all landscape is to some extent part of one 'continuing landscape'.

Some chronological horizons of the landscape, like stages of a building's evolution, can disappear for a time (perhaps for thousands of years) only to reappear in different (perhaps impoverished and devalued) but still legible forms under later land use. It is within this complex interaction of the physical effect of successive land uses, with their preceding landscape remains, that archaeological and other forms of survival, and therefore the

historic landscape itself, will exist. A particular land use may cease, but later start again in identical or similar forms; it can be cyclical, and interleaved with other land uses; it will always experience continual modification to varying degrees up to a scale of change at which the archaeological remains might suggest discontinuity, or in which no archaeology can survive.

The principles set out here for general adoption also emphasise the chronological continuity of the landscape more than its separate historical or period-based episodes – 'the whole not the parts' argument, used here in terms of time and chronology rather than of features and space. An approach which isolates a single-period landscape from its chronological context, or which identifies the 'best' examples of a typology, will ignore this time-depth, which English Heritage identifies as one of the prime attributes of the English landscape. Such an approach may, for example, devalue later changes in the landscape in order to highlight the oldest (or vice versa). If anything has been learned from the early history of conservation, it is surely the need to avoid the trap of anachronistic, 'time-sliced' repair in order to attempt the recreation of a presumed original form.

For these reasons, the English Heritage approach rejects the terms 'relict', 'continuing' or 'period' landscape. Their use sets up obstacles to a sensible understanding and conservation of the historic dimension of the landscape. Instead we begin with the present landscape, and not with the reconstruction of earlier phases or definition of parts of the historic landscape as tangible things that can be catalogued or listed in the same way as simpler sites or buildings. The drawing up of a selected register (which works for definable objects and discrete sites, using all-encompasing systems of classification) is not an appropriate way to manage the whole landscape. It would not provide for local distinctiveness, nor enable communities to form their own informed view on value. It would not allow the flexibility of management and conservation which is necessary both to reflect local circumstances and to leave room for continuity of change. It would, finally,

underplay the great complexity and variety of the landscape.

Positive management

The historic landscape requires a much wider and more flexible response than trying to select simply the 'best sites'. It needs continued active management as much as protection if it is to survive in good condition. Its conservation needs to be applicable at varying scales, and to be subject to current and changing practical needs. It needs to take account of the complexity and variety involved in understanding and assessing the landscape, with its infinite range of types and combinations of landscape features. It also needs to achieve co-ordination with other overlapping conservation values, in order to influence the active land use and management which is essential to conservation.

As well as underlying English Heritage methods, this desire to understand the whole landscape in historic terms is a guiding principle of the Council of Europe recommendation R(95)9 on the conservation of cultural landscape (Johannson 1994, Council of Europe 1995), which in its turn has helped to shape the emerging *European Landscape Convention* (CLRAE 1998). Recommendation R(95)9 states that policies for the conservation of the cultural landscape should be set within the context of general landscape policy, alongside visual and ecological considerations. It defines cultural landscape as the product of the combined action over time of both natural and human factors, a product that testifies to the past and present relationships between people and their environment, and which moulds local culture and diversity. It recommends as a starting point the comprehensive analysis of the whole landscape, whether at local, regional, national, or international level, which thereafter gives a basis for attempting positive management for the whole landscape, not the rigid protection of some of its parts. This is also the primary objective of the work sponsored by English Heritage reported in Part II and the conclusions set out in Part III below.

Fig 14: Cotswolds

PART II: THE HISTORIC LANDSCAPE PROJECT 1992–94

4: Introduction to the project

Andrew McNab

Project objectives

The *Historic Landscape Project* was a programme of research and methodological study commissioned by English Heritage from Cobhams Resource Consultants (CRC) and Oxford Archaeological Unit (OAU) to investigate methods of defining historic landscape, in order to allow proper attention to its conservation. The objectives of it were threefold:

- to identify, produce documentation to tender for, and then to manage a series of developmental experimental research projects ('pilot schemes') which could form the basis of future methodologies for the definition of landscapes of historic importance

- to ensure that these pilot projects covered a diversity of circumstances (such as scale, location, agency, topography, and land use)

- to draw together the results of the pilots in the form of a report comparing the methods, approaches, and results

Four pilot projects were undertaken to inform the work with an understanding of current practice and to explore a number of areas for developing best practice. Two of the projects reviewed current practice:

- a review of historic landscape surveys at the parish, estate, and farm level, carried out by Wessex Archaeology (*see chapter 5*)

- a review of historic landscape assessment in Environmental Statements, carried out by RPS Clouston (*see chapter 6*)

The other two projects were experimental, looking at different regions of England from two perspectives: (*see Fig 15*)

- The identification of historic landscape in Oxfordshire, carried out by Paul Chadwick of Lawson Price, with Della Hooke (*see Fig 15 and chapter 7*)

- The identification of historic landscape in County Durham, carried out by Chris Blandford Associates with South Eastern Archaeological Services and the Oxford Archaeological Unit (*see Fig 15 and chapter 8*)

Background to the project

Cobham Resource Consultants approached the work with the understanding that English Heritage is concerned to conserve not only individual sites of archaeological and historic interest but also the wider archaeological and historic environment. The project brief given to CRC is reproduced at annex 3

In the National Heritage Act of 1983 the Historic Buildings and Monuments Commission for England (English Heritage) was empowered to '... compile a register of gardens and other land situated in England and appearing to them to be of special historic interest.' This provision had already been used to compile a national *Register of Parks and Gardens of Special Historic Interest in England* and, more recently, a *Register of Historic Battlefields*. In its book *Ancient monuments in the countryside* (Darvill 1987), however, a first attempt was made by English Heritage to relate the survival and management of individual archaeological sites to their wider context in the landscape, by using broad land-cover types: wetlands, coastlands and estuaries, rivers and lakes, old pasture, arable land, woodland, lowland heaths, parks and gardens, and upland moors. In 1990, the Government in its environmental strategy, *This common inheritance* (DoE 1990), invited English Heritage to 'prepare a register of landscapes ...which have historic significance but where there are no longer any identifiable remains.' (DoE 1990, 128, para 9.13). It was suggested that such a register would be informative and would have no legal effect.

In response to the White Paper invitation, English Heritage issued *The historic landscape: an English Heritage policy statement* (Fairclough 1991). This set out the basic principles summarised in chapter 1 above, which any register, or alternative method of approaching the conservation of historic landscape, would have to embrace.

N

Fig 15: Location of regional study areas. County Durham; shaded areas show the extent of the areas studied (see chapter 8 and Fig 23), Oxfordshire; light tone shows study area and dark tone the sample areas (see chapter 7 and Fig 18), and Kent; sample areas shaded (see annex 1 and Fig 33.)

0   50km

Subsequently English Heritage produced *Register of landscapes of historic importance: a consultation paper* (English Heritage 1991d written by David Morgan-Evans) on the proposed register of landscape of historic importance. This discussed the potential use of a register, drawing attention to:

- the opportunities for protecting and managing the historic landscape provided by the then-new Countryside Commission's Stewardship Programme and by the Ministry of Agriculture's Environmentally Sensitive Areas

- the consideration already given to historic landscape in some existing designations such as Conservation Areas and Areas of Outstanding Natural Beauty

- the importance of historic landscape in Development Plans and development control

- voluntary efforts to conserve the historic landscape

- the inappropriateness of scheduling to protect extensive tracts of living countryside

The consultation sought consensus on how to define landscapes of historic importance, restricting the definition to the countryside and to the man-made landscape, although mainly excluding non-material cultural associations, or specific features such as historic buildings and parks and gardens, which can be protected by other means.

The definition was established to include the following elements of the historic landscape:

- sub-surface features
- earthworks
- structures and ruins
- roofed structures
- field boundaries
- historic natural features

In relation to the evaluation of historic landscape, the consultation paper outlined a simple hierarchical grading, from national importance, through regional importance, to local importance, with an additional category for areas or components of residual significance (eg non-historic/destroyed). It was suggested that the criteria for assessing national importance could be the same as those used by the Secretary of State for ancient monuments (namely, period, rarity, documentation, group value, survival/ condition, fragility/vulnerability, diversity, and potential), despite the need in such systems for the use of scoring techniques not well suited to the complexity of the whole landscape.

In characterising the historic landscape, the consultation paper rejected a national classification of historic landscape, at least at that stage. The rejection was based upon the complexity of historic landscape and the likelihood of any such classification emphasising single period-sites rather than chronological depth. Alternatively therefore an approach based upon the identification, evaluation, and aggregation of individual historic features was favoured.

The 1991 consultation paper concluded by recommending a pilot project to test alternative methods of historic landscape assessment. This report arises directly from that recommendation. It was not however the only research commissioned at this time by English Heritage to investigate methods of historic landscape assessment. Two other initiatives (described below) also formed an important part of the background to the project.

English Heritage had already begun to participate in the *New Map of England Pilot Project* initiated by the Countryside Commission (Countryside Commission 1994b), which developed into the *Countryside Character Map* compiled jointly by the Countryside Commission and English Nature with help from English Heritage (*see chapter 2* and Countryside Commission 1998 and Agency 1999). This pilot project was designed to identify distinctive landscape at a regional or sub-regional scale. The pilot project (which related to south-west England) was almost complete at the time that English Heritage's *Historic Landscape Project* was undertaken.

The English Heritage contribution to the earlier joint project had been to commission Della Hooke, working with Land Use Consultants (LUC), to prepare data on the historic landscape of the region. This work included a subdivision of the region into historic areas and sub-areas based largely on enclosure history, and based primarily upon the use of primary and secondary documentary sources. Della Hooke applied a similar technique to another area as part of the pilot projects described in chapter 6 and below.

A further initiative was a study undertaken in Kent for English Heritage by Paul Chadwick, then of Lawson Price, to devise and test scoring-based methods of historic landscape assessment (*see annex 1*). The study examined a sample of six 25sq km areas selected to represent a range of landscape (*see Fig 15*). Six categories of data were examined to identify historic features as defined by the classification suggested in the English Heritage 1991 consultation paper,(and summarised above). Each feature was evaluated using a numerical scoring system based upon the Secretary of State's criteria for assessing ancient monuments, and the scores were summed for each kilometre grid square, (*see Fig 34 and Tables 8–10*) thus producing a comparative measure for some aspects of the historic landscape. This study is described in detail in annex 1; in general terms, its results supported the view that less qualitative and less component-led approaches were needed.

The wider context of the English Heritage project includes the work supported by ICOMOS on the identification of landscape of cultural importance in Wales. Cadw (English Heritage's sister organisation in Wales) and the Countryside Council for Wales had recently begun preliminary work for the *Welsh Register of Historic Landscape* (Kelly 1994, and Cadw 1998). This work included definition of principles for historic landscape assessment. and was intended both to inform a broad approach to historic landscape assessment and, in the shorter term, to enable the identification of criteria for inclusion in a planned register of historic landscape. This was initially approached by collating the opinions of experts, who were invited to identify a list of their personally-valued areas. This was followed by the preparation of a short evaluation of the archaeological and historical significance of each area. A discussion paper on historic landscape evaluation (Kelly 1993) defined several different attributes of historic landscape, including landscape characteristics of one period, landscape of historic diversity or coherence, landscape with cultural associations, and landscape that had been subsumed or buried. Different evaluation criteria were suggested for each type of landscape. The first product of the work was the publication of a set of archaeological character descriptions for thirty-six discrete areas of 'outstanding historic interest', published in the form of a register, as a set of exemplars (Cadw, 1998). A further publication will provide a second tranche of areas of 'special' historic interest.

Methodology

This section describes the way in which the *Historic Landscape Project* was undertaken, the selection of the pilot projects, their management, the complementary consultations, and the methods by which the results were collated. The main work of the project was undertaken between May and December 1993, the results being presented to English Heritage in a formal report (CRC and OAU 1993) and through a seminar in March 1994 in Savile Row for EH staff and specialist colleagues from other national agencies, local government, and universities.

The project had five principal elements:

- initial review of the subject
- identification of suitable pilot projects
- selection of contractors
- management of the projects
- distillation of findings

Initial review

This element of the work involved a series of rapid reviews of the current situation:

Stage 1: a review of the uses of historic landscape assessment

Stage 2: a review of responses to English Heritage's Consultation Paper

Stage 3: a literature review to identify key issues

Stage 4: a review of practical experience of historic landscape assessment.

Results were summarised in a preliminary project discussion paper, written to provide the explicit theoretical starting point for the main project.

Stage 1 was to review again the range of uses for historic landscape assessment, as a fundamental first step to defining appropriate methods. The primary purpose of historic landscape assessment was taken as being to enhance understanding of the environment. It could be required to inform

Development Plans, take decisions on planning applications and land management, to aid the design of development proposals (through environmental assessment) or simply to promote informed understanding and enjoyment of a local landscape. As such historic landscape assessments will be used by planners, countryside agencies, land managers, landowners, local amenity groups, and other individuals. This suggests that assessment methods will need to be applicable to a variety of scales of landscape from the regional and sub-regional scale (for strategic planning purposes, for example) to the more local scale of parish, estate, or smaller units of land, such as individual farms, for detailed land management purposes. It was resolved that the pilot projects should try to embrace this variety of purpose and scale, covering both policy making and land use and management decisions.

Stage 2, a review of the responses to English Heritage's 1991 consultation paper, was particularly intended to identify views on assessment methodologies. Two different approaches were advocated by respondents, in almost equal proportion. These were a *top-down* approach and a *bottom-up* approach. A *top-down* approach may be characterised as utilising professional expertise to identify areas of historic landscape importance. Several respondents suggested the prior classification of historic landscape types to aid selection. A *bottom-up* approach may be characterised as assembling information about individual historic landscape features and then through a process of scoring, aggregation, and professional judgement, to identify historic landscape character. It was resolved that the pilot projects should include both *top down* and *bottom up* approaches.

Stage 3 a literature review confirmed that an extensive bibliography existed about historic landscape, but little of the material available at the time of the review related to techniques suitable for helping with landscape conservation.

Stage 4 was a rapid review of current practice for historic landscape assessment. It embraced local planning authority practice in relation to Development Plans, the Countryside Commission practice in Area of Outstanding Natural Beauty landscape assessments and that of archaeologists working at estate or farm level.

The results of these first reviews were brought together in a preliminary discussion paper with an initial theoretical overview of the project. This paper was prepared by George Lambrick to inform the early stages of the project, promote discussion within the study team and its Steering

Group, and to guide the pilot projects. It set out initial ideas on definitions, scope, and practical approaches to historic landscape assessment, and made a first attempt to define key terms and classify time-frames and features. It identified possible alternative approaches, reviewed data sources and information needs, examined techniques of characterisation and evaluation, and reviewed uses and implementation. It was updated, amplified, and modified as the overall project proceeded, and forms the basis of the final project report in the following chapters and this present summary.

The review stages were not comprehensive but were of value in informing discussion of issues and in particular allowed the project team to identify key issues and principles, on the basis of which the pilot studies could be designed and commissioned.

Identification of the pilot projects

The initial reviews described above, in conjunction with the project brief, (*see annex 3*) allowed pilot project proposals to be formulated. These projects were intended to be related to potential user needs, particularly the need to identify important historic landscape at a national, regional, or county level. They were aiming to assist planning and policy formulation and, through practical casework, to address the need to evaluate historic landscape at more local levels such as parish or estate (or even site level) in order to assist land management and environmental assessment. The pilot projects were designed to test different types of approach to assessment, particularly expert judgement, desk-based analysis, and field survey. Finally the pilot projects needed to assess the capability of different professions and organisations to undertake historic landscape evaluation. Four projects were identified: two at county level looking at national/regional scales (*see chapters 5 and 6*) and two at more local levels (*see chapters 7 and 8*).

Two of the projects were designed to assess the feasibility of identifying historic landscape at a county level by carrying out new work. This scale was selected as the most appropriate and the most likely level of policy making. Two counties, Oxfordshire and Durham, were chosen to devise and test the application of different approaches in different environments (*Fig 15 see also chapters 7 and 8*). The second two projects (*see chapters 5 and 6*) were concerned with evaluating work already carried out by others in parish, estate, or farm surveys and in environmental assessment. All the studies were required to consider the range and cost-effectiveness of different techniques.

The Oxfordshire study, (*chapter 7*) which was restricted to the Cherwell, Vale of White Horse and West Oxfordshire Districts, was selected as a lowland county with considerable known archaeological and historic interest. The Durham study, (*chapter 8*) which was defined to include the Districts of Durham, Easington, and the Wear Valley, was selected to provide upland, industrial, and coastal landscape.

The projects had four main objectives:

*   to test two contrasting approaches to historic landscape assessment (expert judgement and desk-based analysis) and to compare the cost effectiveness of both

*   to identify and characterise representative landscape of historic value within the study area

*   to consider whether boundaries or grading of zones of particular interest can be defined

*   to assess the types and extent of data required to establish a robust identification and characterisation of historic landscape.

For both studies the brief required both a *top down* and a *bottom up* approach to be conducted independently.

The two other studies (*see chapters 5 and 6*) were again designed to cover a range of landscape types and were intended to explore, in more detail, the experience derived from different professional disciplines. In both cases a wide range of studies was subjected to an initial appraisal, from which a small number was selected for detailed review. The environmental assessment project was also intended to establish the extent to which historic landscape was covered in current environmental assessments and to consider the views of local planning authorities.

The selection of contractors

In selecting contractors a deliberate attempt was made to use a wide range of skills, experience, professions, and approaches. Thus invitations to tender were made to multi-disciplinary consultancies, archaeological units, academics, and local authorities. Unfortunately, given the tight timescale, a number of academics and each of the local authorities felt unable to tender. This potential shortcoming was overcome by arranging consultation meetings with key academics and local authorities independently of, but in parallel with, the pilot projects. As a result of the tendering process, contracts were issued as follows :

Farm surveys: Wessex Archaeology (*chapter 5*)

Environmental assessments: RPS Clouston (*chapter 6*)

Oxfordshire: Lawson-Rice with Della Hooke (*chapter 7*)

County Durham: Chris Blandford Associates with South Eastern Archaeological Services (*chapter 8*)

Management of the projects

CRC project officers oversaw each pilot project. Regular liaison meetings were held, progress reports were prepared and the project officers attended field meetings with each of the study teams. Draft final reports from each of the pilot projects were reviewed by the main project team and formed the basis for discussion with the

Steering Group comments were fed back to each of the contractors prior to the preparation of the final reports.

Distillation of findings

Apart from a detailed review of the pilot project reports, which led to the preparation of a draft report on the project, the principal means of distilling the findings was an EH seminar held in autumn 1993 at Regent's College, London, attended by the project team and its Steering Committee, the subcontractors, and invited guests. The morning was devoted to presentation and discussion of the four pilot project; the afternoon to a broad-based discussion of key issues. The project's final report to EH (CRC and OAU 1993), of which chapters 4–10 of the present book represent the published summary, was finalised. in the light of this seminar. The findings of the project were also presented to an EH seminar held at 23 Savile Row in March 1994. The next four chapters summarise the results of each of the pilot projects. The earlier project in Kent summarised above is described in annex 1

5: Local landscape surveys at parish or estate level

Richard Newman

This study was undertaken by Wessex Archaeology. It was designed to review and assess the merits of various historic assessment methodologies used by parish and estate-based historic landscape surveys completed before 1993. Two tasks were identified by the brief:

- the review and classification of a range of parish/estate surveys of historic landscapes in England in order to identify five surveys for detailed study, and

- the evaluation of the five chosen surveys to enable justified recommendations on best practice for future surveys.

Surveys at this scale were selected for study because one of the main contexts for landscape-scale work in recent years has been work at farm, parish, or estate scale, partly through local government funded work such as the Englishcombe, Avon survey and through English Heritage's own grants programme for *Farm Surveys*. These surveys were also relevant to the aims of the historic landscape project because one of their main objectives was to improve conservation and management of the historic dimension of landscape by creating a better understanding of what should be saved. To develop sensible conservation management strategies requires a sound knowledge of the landscape's historic resource and its relevance.

Methodology

It was considered essential that a full range of historic landscape studies of parishes and estates was reviewed. These were if possible to cover the work of archaeologists, historic ecologists, historical geographers, landscape architects, landscape historians, and palaeo-environmentalists. Thirty-five surveys were reviewed initially (listed in Table 1) in order to provide a sufficiently wide sample A few parts of the country were not represented (notably East Anglia and also much of the North) despite attempts to achieve an even geographical distribution.

The most obvious difficulty to be overcome in appraising a wide range of historic landscape surveys was to establish a mechanism which would allow an objective comparison of these thirty-five studies. To achieve this forms were

devised which allowed the scoring of surveys according to their coverage of set categories. There were twenty-four categories dealing with the landscape aspects, the application of grading systems, and the general usefulness of the surveys. The relative weight given in any particular study to each of the categories was dependent on the purpose of the study and on the area of expertise of the study's researchers. A scoring system was used to create a means of comparative assessment of the initial surveys.

A selection of five studies for more detailed evaluation was made from the ten top scoring studies. This selection process also took into account factors such as location, survey types, practitioners, and survey areas. A detailed review of each survey chosen was undertaken, measuring the extent to which each survey covered the full range of all historic elements of the landscape including semi-natural features, approached the relative weighting of landscape of greater or lesser significance, and offered a method of taking account of individual features of a landscape for day-to-day management by landowners, tenants or other bodies charged with site management (English Heritage 1991d).

Interviews were conducted with the team leaders and/or report authors of the five chosen surveys, using a set questionnaire. The questions asked concentrated on those aspects of each of the surveys which had not been fully covered in the original survey reports. Questions were particularly targeted at establishing resource levels, both financial and manpower. The questionnaire was also designed to investigate the survey practitioners own assessment of their surveys value, its contribution to an understanding the landscape, and how well it met its own stated objectives. Finally it sought to establish whether the survey practitioners considered with hindsight that improvements could have been made to their survey methodology.

Results of analysis of initial sample

Types and classification of assessment approaches

The types of historic landscape assessments of parishes and estates which had been carried out varied greatly. This variety related to two principle factors: the purpose of the assessment and the professional backgrounds of the assessment leaders. Some of the assessments reviewed were undertaken for academic research, others as parts of environmental impact assessments, or for planning purposes, still others as precursors to management plans or as part of grant application packages. Most assessments were undertaken by archaeologists, historical geographers, landscape architects, or local historians. Other professions had been involved as specialist advisors, and had occasionally acted as head of a survey team. These included arboriculturalists, botanists, ecologists, horticulturalists, and palaeo-environmentalists.

The Cadw/Countryside Commission for Wales *Historic landscape project in Wales* defined four basic approaches to recording historic landscape; quantitative, period based, total feature recording, and classification (Kelly 1993). This categorisation can be refined into a division by mode of classification and analytical approach.

Classification:
- **Period based**: analysis of landscape through the selection of features by period eg prehistoric, Roman, medieval

- **Typological**: analysis of landscape through selection by type eg enclosure, landscaped park, industrial

- **Total feature**: review of all features in the landscape irrespective of derivation or date

Analytical approach:
- **Descriptive**: the systematic collation and presentation of data to form a coherent and cogent narrative explanation of the landscape's development. This level is the basis of all studies

- **Quantitative**: the division and sorting of the landscape into components and into distinct areas with definable and recognisable characters in accordance with set criteria

- **Qualitative**: the evaluation of a landscape qualities through attaching value by reference to set criteria

All historic landscape assessments will equate with at least one of these modes of classification and one of these analytical approaches, but none are exclusive. A total feature approach to the landscape may involve a presentation of results which subdivides the findings according to period or typology or both. The quantitative and the qualitative analytical levels both require a

descriptive level as an initial basis, and the qualitative approach usually also needs a level of quantitative analysis before it can be applied. The analytical levels defined are broadly similar to the stages of assessment process as described by the Countryside Commission, involving landscape description, classification and evaluation (Countryside Commission 1993, 4).

In general historic landscape assessments are undertaken for reasons of interest and research, or carried out as part of a conservation or management-linked commission, and frequently for both reasons. Research-led surveys are often typological or period based in type and usually descriptive. Conservation-led surveys favour either the period based or total feature approach and are usually quantitative and occasionally qualitative. Surveys that seek to establish the relative weighting of the importance of landscape components need to be comprehensive in their coverage of these elements and both quantitative and qualitative in analysis.

The initial review

A total of 35 surveys (*see Fig 16 and Table 1*) were chosen as the sample for preliminary review.

The sample was largely based on accessibility, and the range was unavoidably uneven geographically, professionally, and methodologically. Nevertheless, examples of all the categories identified in the brief were considered. The sample included both upland and lowland, inland and coastal sites and a diversity of geological and soil types. The sample was largely biased towards Southern and Midland England.

Of the thirty-five surveys reviewed twenty-seven (77%) were carried out by archaeologists or historians, seven (20%) by landscape architects or land surveyors and one by an historical geographer. Twelve of the surveys had been completed by the National Trust, in nearly all cases using archaeologists or historians as the team leaders supported by specialists including botanists and arboriculturalists. The most recent National Trust surveys used had followed standardised guidelines formulated by their archaeological advisers (National Trust 1992).

There is a clear division in the nature of the work undertaken and of the professions involved between designed ornamental landscape and non-designed landscape. Designed landscape surveys tend to have been carried out by landscape architects as part of commissioned assessments (although the National Trust was mainly an exception to this), whereas non-designed landscape assessments were usually undertaken by archaeologists or historians, and

Table 1: Farm and estate-scale historic landscape appraisal, review sample

landscape	county	type	designed landscape	author type
Englishcombe	Avon	Estate	No	Archaeologist
Stoke Park, Bristol	Avon	Estate	Yes	Landscape architects
Widcombe*	Avon	Estate	No	Archaeologist
Cardington & Eastcotts	Beds*	Parish	No	Archaeologist
Chalgrave	Beds	Parish	No	Archaeologist
Shillington	Beds	Parish	No	Archaeologist
Ascott	Bucks*	Estate	No	National Trust
Bradenham	Bucks	Estate	No	National Trust
Mentmore	Bucks	Estate	Yes	Landscape architects
Cambridge Estates	Cambs*	Estate	No	Archaeologist
Dannonchapel Farm	Cornwall	Farm	No	National Trust
Great Langdale*	Cumbria	National park	No	National Trust
Calke Abbey	Derby	Estate	Yes	National Trust
Castle Hill	Devon	Estate	Yes	Landscape architects
Dartmoor	Devon	National park	No	Archaeologist
Oakhampton	Devon	Estate	No	Archaeologist
Corfe village	Dorset	Estate	No	National Trust
Weld*	Dorset	Estate	No	Archaeologist
Minchinhampton	Gloucs*	Estate	No	National Trust
Old Grange	Gloucs	Estate	Yes	Archaeologist
Mottisfont Abbey	Hants*	Estate	Yes	National Trust
Brockhampton	Here&Worc	Estate	Yes	National Trust
Belton Park Gardens	Lincs*	Gardens	Yes	National Trust
Blenheim	Oxon*	Estate	Yes	Archaeologist
Middleton Stoney	Oxon	Parish	No	Archaeologist
Minehead Without	Somerset	Parish	No	Archaeologist
Barrington Court	Somerset	Estate	Yes	National Trust
Shugborough	Staffs*	Estate	Yes	National Trust
Painshill Park	Surrey	Estate	Yes	Archaeologist
Part Firle*	E Sussex	Estate	No	Land agents
Chichester Harbour	W Sussex	AONB	No	Landscape architects
Morton Bagot	Warwicks	Parish	No	Archaeologist
Whiteparish	Wilts*	Parish	No	Archaeologist
Stonehenge	Wilts	Estate	No	Landscape architects
Plumpton Rocks*	N Yorks	Estate	Yes	Landscape architects

*site surveys selected for detailed study

most frequently undertaken as part of research programmes. The parameters and methodologies therefore. tend to be quite different. All seven of the parish surveys reviewed were carried out by archaeologists, historians, or historical geographers, as part of research programmes, although those carried out by Bedfordshire County Council's archaeologists were also compiled for planning purposes. Generally it has not been part of the remit of parish surveys to define, classify, or grade historic landscape. It is probably because of this difference in purpose that parish surveys, despite their often excellent academic content, scored on average less highly than estate surveys. No parish surveys were ranked higher than of standard quality.

The principal scores for professional groups were summed and mean scores estimated. The groups were the National Trust, landscape architects or land surveyors, archaeologists or historians, and historical geographers. Work by the National Trust had a sufficiently distinctive character (in terms of consistency of methods and aims) to merit treatment as a separate professional group.

Professional mean scores:

Archaeologists/historians/ historical geographers	72
Landscape architects/surveyors	74
National Trust	66

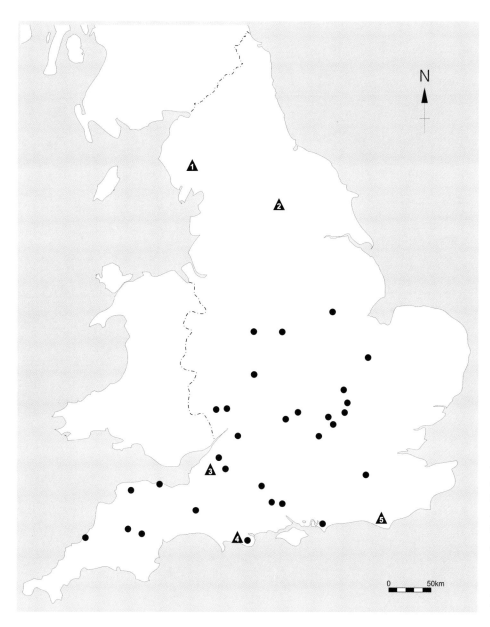

Fig 16: Location of the 35 farm and estate surveys used; no 1 Great Langdale, Cumbria; no 2 Plumpton Rocks, North Yorkshire; no 3 Widcombe, Avon; no 4 Weld, Dorset; no 5 Part Firle, East Sussex; (see Table 1 for complete list)

All the scores fall in the range defined as standard, across a very tight distribution. This suggests, despite differences in approach, that there is no discernible difference in the overall quality of the surveys between the different groups when viewed against the criteria set out for this pilot study. It does not mean, however, that their strengths and weaknesses are the same. It was observable that different categories of data were utilised by the different professional groupings and between surveys of designed and non-designed landscapes.

Some surveys attempted to evaluate the historic importance of an area by qualitative classification or grading The initial sample was therefore assessed in terms of the grading system used. This analysis showed that twenty-five landscape surveys did not include any grading systems, and a further four used systems considered in this assessment to be inadequate. Only three appear to have used a grading system which this review considered to be wholly adequate.

Those surveys which did attempt a grading of historic elements did so largely to aid the management and conservation of individual elements of the landscape rather than to assess the qualities of the historic landscape as a whole. Needless to say, the two are not directly comparable or compatible, but any internal qualitative grading within a defined landscape is likely to be relevant to its overall quality in regional or national terms.

Although few of the surveys rigorously applied any grading system, those that were applied varied in their criteria and in the level of rigour of their application of them. Less than 10% of the surveys reviewed had any adequate attempt to grade within the landscape, and thus only one of the case studies, Weld, Dorset, used a grading system. (Keen and Carreck 1987)

The simplest system involves grading historic elements or components of the landscape and is exemplified by that adopted by the National Trust in their archaeological surveys. They grade recorded archaeological sites as being of local, regional, national importance, or archaeological potential and these are the only elements graded. This approach can be enhanced if more than one category of landscape component (ie archaeological and semi-natural historic features) is graded.

Detailed case studies

Five surveys were chosen for detailed review from the initial sample of thirty-five surveys (Fig 16 and Table 1). These were:

- Great Langdale, Cumbria (Fig 16, no 1, National Trust 1990)
- Plumpton Rocks, North Yorkshire (Fig 16, no 2, The Landscape Practice 1992)
- Widcombe, Avon (Fig 16, no 3, Russett 1988)
- Weld, Dorset (Fig 16, no 4, Keen and Carrick 1989)
- Part Firle, East Sussex (Fig 16, no 5, Strutt and Parker nd)

The five chosen surveys were selected on the basis of a number of criteria. They provided a balanced sample in terms of landscape type, geographical spread, topography, survey method and surveyors' professional background. Other factors that were taken into account included the date of the project (advances in techniques and changes in philosophy discouraged the selection of projects undertaken over a decade ago), ease of access to copies of the survey results, and the availability of survey team leaders for critical comment. Parish surveys were not considered for selection because they are generally undertaken to provide a different sort of landscape study to that required for this review. All these factors combined to ensure that the highest scoring surveys were not in every case those selected for detailed review.

The variety of objectives, approach and scale of the five chosen case studies made it difficult to make certain comparisons. In particular no meaningful comparison of the financial and manpower resources committed could be made because of the varying nature of the projects, their financial arrangements, and the date when they were conducted. The financial resources committed to a Manpower Services Commission scheme, administered by a local authority, could not be meaningfully compared with a landscape architects commission. In terms of manpower

and specialist skills, however, it is clear that skilled multi-disciplinary teams as employed at Plumpton Rocks, North Yorkshire, (Landsape Practice 1992) produce the most satisfactory reports. Equally Manpower Services Commission teams, when led by an experienced landscape archaeologist, did produce good results, but on a lengthy timescale and with costs unlikely to be acceptable to most potential clients. The best presented reports in relation to land management requirements were those prepared by landscape architects and land surveyors, perhaps because of their greater familiarity with commercial imperatives in comparison with local authority archaeologists.

The best reports made a good use of graphic material. Photographic comparisons and attribute-mapping can quickly convey ideas and impressions. The use of colour assists visual interpretation and makes a report more visually appealing. Summarised lists of attributes are useful, as are management recommendations. Such data presentations can be easily copied and used in the field by non-specialists who must attempt to turn management recommendations into physical realities.

Neither the case studies on their own, or even the entire survey sample, are entirely satisfactory as an aid to defining good practice in historic landscape assessments. All the surveys were generally deficient in some respects. In general terms, there was a lack of the use of full-scale archaeological fieldwork, palaeo-environmental studies or integrated ecological studies, or the more sophisticated techniques such as landscape regression analysis and the application of GIS techniques in the surveys reviewed. This partly reflects practice at the time when the surveys were carried out (GIS for example has only recently become commonly available as an analytical tool),. but the quality of the surveys is also at least in part an indication of a lack of uniform methodological definition in historic landscape appraisal.

Overall implications

All the surveys, taken as a group, exhibit some common gaps in coverage. There was often a limited use of ecological data, which until recently was often wholly ignored in historic landscape appraisals (Coones 1985, 7). It is now usually included, but it is not always adequately integrated with other aspects of historic landscape. The practice current amongst some landscape practitioners, of layering separate items of expertly derived data into a report, with little or no attempt at editing or evaluating that data, does not promote ecological integration. Layering is an approach made possible and popular by information technology. This makes superficial analysis easy to produce using simple CAD-based data overlay techniques. Reports can be compiled using specialist's reports supplied as disc files, but this is no substitute for a reasoned and well presented report containing synthesis and interpretation.

In the five surveys reviewed in detail, documentary research and simple landform analysis were usually used, but other basic techniques, such as archaeological walkover surveys and aerial photographic analysis, were not always used. Palaeo-environmental studies were hardly ever undertaken as part of wider landscape surveys, generally being reserved for specialist projects, nor was landscape regression analysis exploited to provide time-depth in the landscape analysis. On the positive side there is an increasing awareness amongst landscape architects of the scientific techniques available, and increasing awareness amongst archaeologists and historians of the need to consult and integrate adequately other specialist work. All landscape practitioners are becoming aware of the benefits of CAD and GIS and their potential for allowing the development of easily updatable management plans.

The quality and subject coverage of the approaches used in the various surveys appeared to be influenced by the parameters of the type of study involved. These were, in turn dictated by the studies intended purposes, rather than by any professional theoretical or methodological preference for one approach instead of another. This is most vividly exposed in a comparison of the approaches of National Trust archaeologists to those of other archaeologists. All are from the same professional background but the approaches adopted in their surveys appear to be markedly different. This difference, as is to be expected, is wholly the result of the different and special agenda to which the National Trust group is working.

Some general strengths could be identified in the main professional groups undertaking historic landscape surveys. Overall archaeologists and historians were stronger on the academic aspects of a landscape study, whereas landscape architects presented their findings more clearly and made better use of visual information. All the professional groups, however, have been disinclined to utilise qualitative methods of analysis and have been engaged in sterile internal professional debates over the advantages and disadvantages of subjective and objective assessment methods.

The task of demonstrating that an area of landscape justifies the distinction of designation as of historic significance (in order to inform management decisions) requires a survey which can demonstrate how the area's historic elements articulate and interrelate, both chronologically and spatially. To do this a staged approach is required, involving landscape classification, characterisations, scoring, and grading. This can only be meaningfully undertaken by the systematic application of consistent appraisal standards, within a national framework of historic landscape character definition.

Historic landscape appraisals require a structured systematic approach which uses all the available data appropriate to the scale of the project. They should be a quantitative and qualitative assessment of the entire historic resource in the landscape being assessed. In the context of this review of parish and estate surveys, there is a general failure to meet these standards which emphasises the need for national standards to be devised agreed and adopted. It is possible that the poor performance noted is in part a result of the date of many of the surveys reviewed, but it is also true that few surveys have been able to subscribe to a commonly-adopted methodology because none has existed. The National Trust surveys are instructive in this respect in view of their adoption of an effective and successful Trust 'house-style', and interviews with landscape practitioners and a review of recent literature show that the whole

Table 2: Parish, estate and farm surveys; data sources and investigative techniques

Source/technique	Great Langdale, Cumbria	Plumpton Rocks, North Yorks	Widcombe, Avon	Weld, Dorset	Part Firle, East Sussex
General documentary research	*	*	*	*	*
Historical documentary research	*	*	-	*	-
SMR	*	-	-	*	*
Air photography	*	-	-	*	-
Land classification	*	-	-	-	*
Field observations	*	*	*	*	-
Detailed site survey	*	-	-	*	-
Hedgerow and boundary surveys	*	*	*	*	-
Ecological surveys	-	-	-	*	-

methodology and discipline is everywhere developing rapidly.

Acknowlegements

The author is grateful to many people who helped with the project. The work itself was carried out with Dr Michael Allen (Wessex Archaeology) who jointly undertook the research and the writing of the original report. The library staffs of the Institute of Advanced Architectural Studies (University of York) and the Landscape Institute provided much valuable help. Finally, the project depended very heavily on the work and advice of David Thackeray (National Trust) and Phil Claris (then National Trust), Lawrence Keen (Dorset County Council), Vince Russet and Mary Stacey (then Avon County Council, now South Gloucestershire and Bath and North East Somerset unitary authorities respectively), Martin Mortimer (The Landscape Practice), James Bridgeland (Strutt and Parker), David Baker (then Bedfordshire County Council, now David Baker Associates) and Stephen Coleman (Bedfordshire County Council).

6: Historic Landscape in Environmental Impact Assessments

David Freke

This study was designed to examine how the identification and protection of historic landscape has been used in the planning process, and specifically in Environmental Statements submitted in support of planning applications under the *European Union Environmental Impact Assessment Directive* (DoE 1988 Planning Circular 15/88 and DoE 1989). Each of the four studies investigated the ways in which the identification, characterisation, evaluation, assessment and protection of historic landscape could be advanced.

The brief for this pilot study required that five environmental statements be studied in detail. It was considered essential that the chosen statements should have completed their progress through the planning processes in order that they could be assessed for their effect on planning decisions. The aim of reviewing this sample was to establish current practice related to historic landscape survey, to review the methods used by different agencies, the resources required (both human and financial) and the effect of historic landscape considerations on Environmental Statement on planning decisions. From this study recommendations as to best practice were to be proposed.

Methodology

The project's main tasks were:

- to review the experience of the evaluation of historic landscape in environmental assessment

- to identify five environmental assessments for detailed study

- review the historic landscape component of each of the five assessments

- to examine the planning authority's approach to appraising historic landscape issues within the environmental assessment

- to recommend on best practice in preparing the historic landscape component

Two environmental statement directories (one prepared by the Impacts Assessment Unit of Oxford Brookes University (Heaney and Therivel 1993), the other by the Institute of Environmental Assessment at Manchester University (unpublished but with annual analysis, Colley and Lee 1990, Lee and Colley 1990,

Jones, Lee and Wood 1991, Wood and Jones 1992) were consulted. It is estimated that by 1993 about 2000 environmental statements had been submitted to planning authorities since 1988 when the relevant planning regulations came into force (DoE planning circular 15/88). Approximately 400 summaries and 100 full environmental statement documents were reviewed in order to select five environmental statements for detailed study. The selection was based on several factors including type of project, location, type of agency carrying out the assessment, and methodology. It became clear at an early stage of the study that only a limited number of environmental statements, particularly those which had completed their passage through the planning system, contained any significant historic landscape element. Other studies which contained useful methodologies or insights were therefore used as supporting documents.

The cultural heritage section of each of the five selected environmental statements was reviewed using a modified version of the method developed by the Environmental Impact Assessment Centre of Manchester University to test conformity with the regulations (Colley and Lee 1990). The four levels of review in the method are arranged hierarchically, from the most detailed elements to an overview. Each element in the hierarchy is ranked from 'well performed' to 'very unsatisfactory' to arrive at an overall assessment of the quality of the individual environmental statement. The selected environmental statements were then reviewed for the range and appropriateness of the techniques used, using a checklist itemising potential methods. An evaluation of the way historic landscape was assessed in each document was also undertaken using a checklist of six hierarchically arranged elements: components, time frames, functional type, spatial relationships, survival, and historic landscape character. Methods of historic landscape evaluation in the selected Environmental Statement were measured against the national non-statutory criteria used by the MPP for scheduling (English Heritage 1997b). The project also reviewed any grading procedures used (eg Goodchild 1990, 47), levels of detail employed, (Lambrick 1993) and of the study and the skills and resources used. The planning authority's response was also reviewed, and an attempt made to assess the effect of the historic landscape component of the Environmental Statement on the outcome of the planning application.

Fig 17: Location of Environmenal Assessment surveys reviewed: no 1 Cragg Quarry, Northumberland; no 2 Pode Hall Farms, Cambridgeshire; no 3 Passenham, Northamptonshire; no 4 Stonehenge Visitor Centre, Wiltshire; no 5 A27 Worthing to Lancing, Sussex; a The Hadrian's Wall National Trail, Cumbria and Northumberland; b The Towcester Retail Development Response, Northamptonshire; c The National Rivers Authority: Oxford Flood Plain, Oxfordshire; d The Broad Oak Reservoir Study, Kent

General review of historic landscape assessments

The summary study of approximately 25% of all Environmental Statements revealed that only in very few cases had historic landscape assessment been undertaken as part of the statements; only eighteen being identified in the consultation and scanning process. However, historic landscape issues are a comparatively recent concern and the need to review only Environmental Statement that had passed through the planning processes meant that more recent studies could not be included in the review.

Review of the types of development project in which cultural heritage impact was considered demonstrated, unsurprisingly, that mineral extraction was one of the most common mentioned in the list of environmental statements with heritage studies, whereas landfill projects hardly figured at all. Some projects, such as cross-

country power lines, should also probably figure more strongly than they do in practice. The geographical distribution of environmental statements generally showed a preponderance in the south-east and midlands and a paucity in the north and west, reflecting predictable regional patterns of development. The types of project also reflected geographical factors, with industry, mineral extraction, and agriculture predominating in the north; wind farms in the south-west, and business, residential, and transport projects in the south.

The range of agencies undertaking cultural heritage contributions to environmental statements was noted. Often the lead consultants were planning or engineering practices, few of which had in-house environmental practitioners. Many specialist environmental reports are provided by subcontractors who may be part of an integrated environmental team. The range of skills needed to assess the historic landscape is usually outside the scope of any one individual or specialism, as it embraces ecology, architecture, geography, documentary history, archaeology, and landscape architecture. A team approach is usually considered the most effective, although the co-ordination of teamwork has often been lacking. Specialists were frequently engaged on the same project, but they rarely had any contact with one another.

The level of historic landscape study was very variable, with the initial scoping of the studies often poorly established. Some of the more thorough assessments were in areas or involved topics where national or regional research programmes were already under way. The data collection methodologies used in the selected studies ranged from document-based to fieldwork-based, but all shared a more or less-detailed *bottom-up* approach. The methods used to identify and assess historic landscape were variable, ranging from intuitive judgements to quantitative comparisons. The methodologies in use for grading, or for making assessments of historic landscape quality, where any were actually attempted, tended to be adapted from the MPP and Listed Building criteria. Ranking was hardly attempted, and there was no agreed scoring or assessment system.

Selected case studies

The five selected case studies were:

- Cragg Quarry, Northumberland (Fig 17, no1)
- Pode Hall Farms, Cambridgeshire (Fig 17, no 2)
- Passenham Quarry, Northamptonshire (Fig 17, no 3)
- Stonehenge Visitor Centre, Wiltshire (Fig 17, no 4)
- A27 Worthing to Lancing, Sussex (Fig 17, no 5)

Cragg Quarry, Northumberland: a mineral extraction project, undertaken for a private developer by a local consultancy, Heritage and Landscape Surveys Limited, whose work has a fieldwork and historic basis. The methodology included a system for expressing the sequences of historic features in the form of a matrix. Practitioners using such an approach require a high degree of training. The site was small and the study very detailed, incorporating a field assessment of all man-made features, including modern ones. The study did not attempt the assessment of below ground features, nor any scoring of the features which were identified. The development proposal was approved, indicating that the study demonstrated to the satisfaction of the planning authority either that no significant cultural heritage features were likely to be affected, or that any impacts could be satisfactorily mitigated.

Pode Hall Farms, Cambridgeshire: a mineral (sand and gravel) extraction project, the assessment was carried out for a private developer by an independent archaeological contractor, the Fenland Archaeological Trust. The peat and wetland aspect of this study was an important consideration. The principal targets of the survey were Roman field systems and buried prehistoric material. The historic landscape element of the Environmental Statement included these buried features. The recommendations of the study were accepted by the applicant and priority areas were either avoided by the proposals or excavation procedures were agreed. The revised application was granted permission by the planning authority.

Passenham Quarry, Northamptonshire: another mineral extraction project. The assessment was carried out by a county council based unit, Northamptonshire Archaeology, after the historic landscape issue had been specifically identified by the planning authority. The range of techniques used in the study includes ecological and historic sources as well as archaeological survey techniques. The survey did not consider alternative sites, and this became an issue at planning appeal against the local authority's refusal of planning permission. In the original refusal decision, the county council's historic landscape policy was invoked. The Planning Inspector's recommendation was for permission with the qualified exclusion of part of the area.

Stonehenge, Wiltshire: proposed site for a visitor centre, undertaken for English Heritage. This was a cultural resource management project overseen by an independent consultant, Professor Tim Darvill, co-ordinating a team of specialists using all available survey techniques. The project was able to use several recent major research studies directed toward both the site itself and its environs. It was a clear and thorough review of the known archaeology, complemented by field evaluations of the potentially affected areas. Alternative sites were less well considered. The historic landscape approach taken was to map all known archaeological features and review easily accessible historic sources, mainly to produce a regression analysis. Scoring was used at monument level but was not extended to the assessment of the historic landscape quality. The planning authority's refusal of planning permission, partly on historic landscape grounds, reflected the high profile of this site and many other factors weighed heavily, not least the agreed desirability of ensuring a full national debate. The existing work that Wiltshire County Council had carried out on Salisbury Plain Training Area, using their own sophisticated methodology for assessing groups of monuments, was also relevant.

A27 Worthing to Lancing, Sussex, road improvements: a road improvement scheme assessment carried out by an independent archaeological contractor, the Oxford Archaeological Unit, for the Department of Transport. A full battery of data collection and evaluation techniques was used, and the assessment was well integrated into an overall historic landscape assessment. This was based on the aggregation of all the data, scored using MPP criteria and judged on a three point scale to produce an 'historic landscape integrity' assessment. All the alternative routes were assessed to the same level. Several research projects related to the area or equivalent areas were quoted by the study. The scheme was still being considered at a public inquiry when this study was undertaken, but the county council and three out of four district councils involved supported it.

Additional studies reviewed

Four additional studies, which did not fully conform to the brief but exhibited aspects of recent approaches useful for the overall study, were also reviewed (Fig 17a-d).

The Hadrian's Wall National Trail, Cumbria and Northumberland: this study was mainly concerned with the survival and vulnerability of archaeological features, and a risk assessment of the likely impact of continuing and/or increased visitor pressure. The study attempted to classify both archaeological features and landforms in order to quantify the vulnerability of each feature. The study introduced rigorous methods for assessing these elements of the historic landscape (Fig 17a).

The Towcester Retail Development Response, Northamptonshire: was chosen because it was an example of a project where the curator was in dispute about the historic landscape setting of a development proposal and because it considered the importance of precise briefs and contributed to the debate about what constitutes the setting of an historic landscape (Fig 17b).

The National Rivers Authority: Oxford Flood Plain, Oxfordshire: this study is relevant because it considers not only all the usual archaeological resources but also documentary, ecological, academic, and aesthetic criteria, operating over a wide landscape area, including buried and modern features as well as visible historic material (Fig 17c).

The Broad Oak Reservoir Study, Kent: was an example of a multi-disciplinary survey carried out by a variety of agencies co-ordinated and monitored in a highly structured fashion, and prioritised with reference to the other elements of the environmental study. An eminent 'auditor' was responsible for overseeing the cultural heritage studies (Fig 17d).

Results

The level of historic landscape assessment in recent environmental statements was generally low, with very few addressing the topic directly. The increasing concern about these issues appears to be leading to an increase in the number of environmental statements which include historic landscape issues, and as development plans begin to include policies (English Heritage *et al* 1996) which specifically refer to historic landscape this trend can be expected to continue.

The strengths and weaknesses of the individual practitioners tended to influence the scope of the surveys. Some practitioners were no doubt chosen because of their particular abilities, but better scoping in briefs and specifications would probably increase the consistency of the surveys and widen their range. Most agencies currently undertaking cultural heritage surveys for environmental statements would be capable of carrying out historic landscape surveys with the involvement of landscape and botanical specialists. A general weakness of most environmental statements was a lack of co-ordination between specialists, and this was very apparent in cultural heritage studies.

All the environmental statements studied used a *bottom-up* approach to cultural heritage studies, taking components of the landscape and building characterisation and evaluation from an analysis of them. The techniques used by the various agencies were generally divided into desk-top studies and fieldwork. The proportions varied for each site: those with a perceived prehistoric component having a higher level of fieldwork than those with a mainly medieval or later emphasis. Most of the desk-top studies used a combination of primary and secondary data sources which now is virtually the norm. A summary of frequency of use is given in Table 3.

Table 3: Historic landscape in environmental assessment: data sources

Sources used	Cragg Quarry, Northumberland	Pode Hall Farms, Cambridgeshire	Passenham Quarry, Northamptonshire	Stonehenge, Wiltshire	A27 Worthing to Lancing, Sussex
Primary Sources					
Victoria County Histories	*	-	*	*	*
Agricultural histories	*	-	*	*	-
Place name records	*	-	*	*	-
Topographic surveys	*	-	*	*	-
Cartographic surveys	*	-	*	*	*
Land charters	*	-	-	*	-
Surveys and tax returns	*	-	-	*	-
Deeds	*	-	-	*	-
Rentals	*	-	-	*	-
Charter and Hundred rolls	-	-	-	*	-
Lay subsidies	-	-	-	*	-
Inclosure records	-	-	*	*	*
Secondary sources					
Archaeological lists and designations					
Scheduled monuments	-	-	-	-	*
SMR	*	*	*	*	*
Listed buildings	*	-	-	*	*
Local lists of historic buildings	*	-	-	*	*
Register of Historic Parks and Gardens	-	-	-	-	*
Conservation areas	-	-	-	-	*
County/LPA designations	-	-	-	-	*

Principal secondary sources used included:

Archaeology:
   Scheduled monuments
   SMR entries
   County and District designations
   air photographs held by the National Monuments Record at Swindon and Cambridge University
   air photographs held by planning authorities and in other collections
   early maps
   accounts of previous work
   museum accession lists
   archives of excavations
   extant geotechnical information (if available)
   geological memoirs
Built environment:
   Listed building designations
   local lists
   Conservation areas
   early maps
   architectural accounts
Ecology:
   English Nature designations (SSSIs)
   County Naturalist Trust designations
   Tree Preservation Orders
   inventories of Ancient Woodland
   extant parish surveys etc
   early maps

Primary documentary research was rarely undertaken and is less easy to specify. It requires the searching of inventories, catalogues, and other lists of archives, and sometimes the ability to read medieval Latin or palaeography. Archaeological field work took the form of both non-invasive and invasive techniques.

Non-invasive methods include field observation, field walking, geophysics, palaeo-environmental sampling, botanical survey, land-use survey, landform analysis, visual appraisal, and landscape assessment. Invasive methods included digging test pits, trial trenches, and palaeo-environmental test pits. There was frequently no discussion of the reasons for the choice of particular techniques.

The environmental statements were studied to see how they had characterised and evaluated historic landscape. When it was attempted at all, characterisation was either a description of the aggregation of historic landscape components or, more rarely, an analysis was made of the periods represented. Again, the lack of an agreed definition and methodology was apparent. Evaluation was also limited and tended to utilise the English Heritage MPP criteria, although in some cases integrated scoring systems were devised.

Table 4: Historic landscape in environmental assessments: investigative techniques

Sources used	Cragg Quarry, Northumberland	Pode Hall Farms, Cambridgeshire	Passenham Quarry, Northamptonshire	Stonehenge, Wiltshire	A27 Worthing to Lancing, Sussex
Archaeology					
Geophysical survey	-	*	*	*	*
Trial trenching	-	*	*	*	-
Field walking	*	*	*	*	*
Archaeological test pits	-	-	*	*	-
Palaeoenvironmental sampling	-	-	*	*	-
Ridge and furrow survey	-	-	*	-	-
Field observations	*	*	*	-	*
Built environment					
Field observations	*	-	-	*	*
Ecology					
Woodland survey	-	-	-	*	-
Grassland survey	-	-	*	*	-
Hedge survey	-	-	*	-	-
Field observations	-	*	-	-	*
Ecological lists and designations					
Sites of Special Scientific Interest	-	*	-	*	*
Ancient woodland	-	-	-	*	-
County habitat surveys	-	-	-	-	-
Tree preservation orders	-	-	-	-	-
Parish surveys	-	-	-	-	-
County trust designations	-	*	-	*	*
Other sources					
Air photos	*	*	*	*	*
Previous archaeological work	*	-	*	*	*
Archaeological fieldwork	*	*	*	*	*
Ecological fieldwork	-	*	*	*	*

Conclusions

The results of the study allow some general conclusions to be drawn:

Principles: there should be a presumption in Environmental Statement that historic elements will always be present. Historic landscape includes buried landscape whose potential should be assessed. The onus should be on the applicant to demonstrate that an area proposed for development is not valuable in historic landscape terms.

Briefs: historic landscape requirements should be written into model Environmental Statement briefs for use by planning authorities, or their omission fully justified. Any exclusion of the consideration of historic landscape issues in an environmental statement must be justified. The fact of having to explain the decision would in many cases lead to the realisation that there were issues to address.

Specifications: the planning authority, as the curator of the cultural heritage resource, should satisfy itself that specifications are realistic and sufficient to achieve the objectives set out in the brief, and if historic landscape assessment is one of these objectives then appropriate details should be required.

National designation: many of the elements which go to make up the historic landscape already have legislative protection, but designation alone cannot represent the historic landscape.

Planning policy: PPG-16 states that it is the planning authorities' responsibility to protect historic landscape (PPG-16, para 14), but this planning policy guidance note's main thrust was to site-based development-control and throughout the rest of the document the terms 'site', 'monument' and 'archaeological remains' are used. More recently, *Planning and the historic environment* (PPG-15, para 6.2) has set out a useful broad definition of the 'wide historic landscape'. English Heritage has also most recently offered preliminary advice on Local Plan policies (English Heritage *et al* 1996).

Agencies: county units, contracting units, and consultants are all capable of carrying out effective historic landscape assessments. Required qualifications for the personnel involved in the historic landscape parts of Environmental Statements should form part of the specifications and be monitored by the curatorial agency.

Approach: the approach to historic landscape in Environmental Statements because of their relatively small size and scale should normally be a *bottom-up* study which moves by progressive levels of integration to an understanding of the landscape as a whole, characterised in terms of the dates, interrelationships, and functions of its components.

Methods: a standard methodology is required which outlines the stages of a project, the range of sources to be consulted and data to be collected, the range of fieldwork to be considered and the techniques of identification and evaluation. The stages of a project should include: desk-based study embracing the core disciplines; non-invasive and invasive field work; the identification of components and the characterisation of landscape, evaluation, impact assessment, and mitigation proposals.

Identification: The identification phase of an historic landscape assessment is at the level of components. All the elements which contribute to a landscape's historic character, that is all significant man-made features (including modern ones), should be encompassed

Characterisation: the identification of the components and their analysis into phases and functions will enable the characterisation of the historic landscape and its categorisation in terms of time frame, functional type, spatial relationships, survival, and overall character.

Evaluation: models for evaluation based on the MPP criteria have been proposed by Lambrick (1992a and b). The evaluation of historic landscape should be possible within this or a similar structure, but rather than an aggregated score being used, each phase of the landscape

development could be evaluated, in order to identify and prioritise them.

Presentation: The presentation of an assessment should clearly identify the differing levels of study, and the decisions and judgements which have been made. The use of chronological maps is advisable, and overlays are a logical device.

Acknowlegements

The author would like to thank Graham Cadman (Northamptonshire Heritage), Roy Canham (Wiltshire County Council, Archaeology Section), A Coleman (Countryside Commission, Northumberland National Park), A Constanduros (Oakwood Environmental) C Davis (Salisbury District Council) Glen Foard (Northamptonshire Heritage) Prof Peter Fowler (University of Newcastle on Tyne), Dr Charles French (University of Cambridge, Department of Archaeology), Gerry Friell (English Heritage) Mr Jupp (West Sussex County Council, Highways Department), Sam Kidd (Northamptonshire Heritage), George Lambrick (Oxford Archaeology Unit), Lancaster University Archaeology Unit, Peter McCrone (Somerset County Council, Environment Department), John Mills (West Sussex County Council, Planning Department), Northamptonshire County Council, Mineral Department, Mrs Robshaw, (Cambridgeshire County Council, Minerals Department), A Saye, (ERL Northern), Bob Sydes (Cambridgeshire County Council, Archaeology Section), Dr R Therivel (Oxford Brookes University, Impact Assessment Unit), Simon Timms (Devon County Council, Archaeology Department), Adrian Tindale (Cheshire County Council, Conservation Group), Adam Welfare (Heritage Site and Landscape Surveys Lt), Dr John Williams (Kent County Council, Archaeology Department), Marcus Wood (Cobham Resource Consultants).

During the project, both George Lambrick of Oxford Archaeology Unit and Andy McNab of Cobham Resource Consultants assisted me greatly by discussing the scope of the project brief and the progress of the work.

7: Oxfordshire

Paul Chadwick

The Oxfordshire experimental pilot project was carried out principally by the author of this chapter and Della Hooke. The area it was to cover was defined as that within the District Council administrative areas of Cherwell, West Oxfordshire and the Vale of White Horse (*see Fig 18*). The area covered was around 1,880 sq km, The project was one of four carried out as part of the *Historic Landscape Project* in 1993–4.

The project's objectives were those set out in chapter 4. The expert judgement approach was provided by a *top-down* module which sought the views of recognised experts via an introductory documentation pack and, where appropriate, by interview. This was intended to test the practicality of devising a methodology to use to produce a national register of important landscape, an idea which was gaining currency in some circles at the time of the project. This aspect of the project was conducted by Anthony Hitchcott, who is qualified as both an ecologist and a landscape-architect. The desk-based approach, or *bottom-up* module, sought to combine historic land use analysis, undertaken by Dr Della Hooke, with a desk-based assessment of landscape-related data in various national and local data sources undertaken by Paul Chadwick. The two modules of the project were progressed completely independently, with the number, extent and character of the historic landscape not compared until the results of each module were documented and report preparation was well underway. The project was managed by a steering group comprising Marcus Wood of Cobham Resource Consultants and George Lambrick of the Oxford Archaeological Unit (the latter also being one of the experts approached in the *top-down* module).

The study commenced in July 1993 and the final report submitted in November 1993. From an early stage of the project, it became apparent that the need to present the project's results cartographically, and the size and shape of the study area, dictated the scale of the mapped output. Even with a map scale of 1:50,000 two large sheets were required to portray the area. Additionally, and possibly slightly at odds with the project's stated aims, it became apparent after very little preliminary thought that the whole of the landscape is historic. Whilst the character and relative importance of individual areas within that landscape varied enormously, the whole study area had to be assessed.

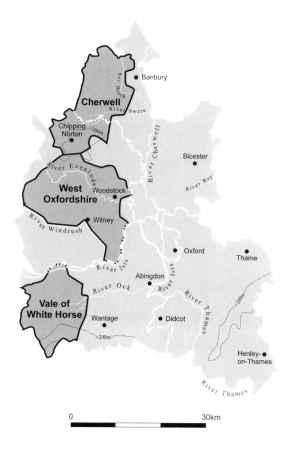

Fig 18: Oxfordshire
(sample areas shown in darker tone)

Top-down approach (using expert judgement)

In the *top-down* module a five stage methodology was proposed. Stage one comprised a review of existing literature, which included Structure and Local Plan designations as well as more general countryside and landscape studies. Approaches in parallel were made to twenty-eight experts identified from an initial literature review and from subsequent recommendation. A series of interviews were then conducted with those who indicated that they were able to take part.

Structured interviews with four experts formed the principal stage of the *top-down* module. Each of these had received briefing documentation comprising the project brief, relevant discussion documents and Ordnance Survey base maps at 1:50,000 showing the study area and administrative boundaries. During the interview phase each participant was asked to:

- identify as far as they were able areas of historic landscape within the study area

- define the principal historic features and elements that characterise those areas

- explain the criteria used in identifying and evaluating each area, and to grade areas so identified

On the basis of these interviews a draft map showing areas of historic landscape was prepared for circulation and review with the contributing experts. Finally, upon completion of this iterative process, report preparation was undertaken, during which a comparison with the results of the *bottom-up* module was made.

It has to be recorded that the *top-down* approach came perilously close to failing completely. Of the twenty-eight experts who had been selected either for their particular specialist area of knowledge, eg topography, or were approached for their broader or more holistic experience of the landscape, almost half did not respond, declined an involvement, or were unable to participate through pressure of time or because the project was operating on a voluntary rather than a fee-paid basis. Of the remainder, a number requested additional information which was discussed at length in an attempt to glean any helpful output, but in the event only four experts actually contributed formal opinions to this module of the project. The approach therefore became very dependent upon the contribution of this small number of inputs, two of which were geographically restricted.

There were considerable variations even between the four submissions which were provided in the level of detail and geographic spread in the historic landscape identified by the expert judgement module. In practice two of the experts resorted to an approach relying exclusively upon primary sources of data, ie site/topic/area specific records within their sphere of expertise. These experts conceded that their specialist viewpoint ran counter to the increasingly holistic approach to historic landscape and made only a modest attempt to further characterise, evaluate, or grade the sites or areas identified. In marked contrast, the geographical coverage and level of detail provided by the two other respondents salvaged this module of the project. The contribution of George Lambrick here is noteworthy. His comprehensive coverage, arising from the premise that all landscape has at least some historic interest or importance, the extent of his

knowledge and his understanding of the project and its objectives was unparalleled among our experts. Indeed, Lambrick was the only expert contributor to characterise, evaluate and grade the landscape identified. This tended to show that an exclusive reliance on the availability of expert advice was not a viable option

Bottom-up approach (desk-based review)

The methodological approach required for the *bottom-up* module was slightly more complex since it had to marry two differing scales of study and analysis. The historic land use study, undertaken by Della Hooke, concentrated on three sample areas comprising *c*35% of the total area (Fig 18). Sample area 1 comprised at least twelve parishes centre around Banbury (Cherwell District), sample area 2 comprised at least twelve parishes centred on the Witney-Woodstock-Wychwood area of West Oxfordshire, and sample area 3 took at least five parishes in the Vale of White Horse.

Fig 19: Oxfordshire: sample area 1 - the Redlands' character area (working map by Della Hooke)

Within these sample areas, with 1:50,000 as the base map scale, the nineteenth-century parish boundaries were reconstructed from Tithe Awards. The parish unit then formed the base for plotting all land use information (*see Fig 19*) and was the principal building block in identifying *Historic Landscape Character Areas*. Manuscript and cartographic sources (eg estate and enclosure maps) allowed a rapid reconstruction of pre-enclosure landscape and demonstrated the extent and form of eighteenth-century villages, farmsteads and road patterns. Early county maps eg Davis (1797) for Oxfordshire and Rocque (1761) for

Berkshire and the Ordnance Survey First Edition (1830–33), then usefully charted contractions in heathland, growth in urbanisation, spread of canals, railways, quarries, and other features. Field validation was limited and concentrated on confirming the relevance of key characteristics and clarifying boundary zones where key characteristics stop, gradually merge into others or cease to be a principal characteristic. The resulting maps (Figs 19, 20, and 21) showing early medieval and medieval land use were prepared and an accompanying report, which included comment on the dynamics of medieval and more recent settlement, trade and communications, across the landscape was prepared for use in the second phase of this module.

The identification of a number of key characteristics for each *Historic Landscape Character Area* was integral and essential to the definition of historic land use areas (Table 5).

The second phase of the *bottom-up* module used these key characteristics in order to extrapolate the historic land use analysis of the sample areas to the remaining 65% of study area. This did not require mental gymnastics or such a leap in methodology or consistency as might be anticipated. Key characteristics were generally matters of observation, rather than supposition (for example: village cores comprise buildings of Corallian Limestone, deer parks absent, or low density, nucleated villages of regular street plan) and defining the full extent of each *Historic Landscape Character Area* was therefore 'merely' a case of defining the full spatial limits of the suite of key characteristics. Six *Historic Landscape Character Areas* were defined, with some of them being further subdivided (*see Fig 22*).

To achieve this the data relevant to each key characteristic was examined, thus if an *Historic Landscape Character Area* was defined by three key characteristics: nucleated villages, limestone building materials, and an absence of deer parks, then information from Davis' 1797 Map of Oxfordshire (showing a pictorial representation

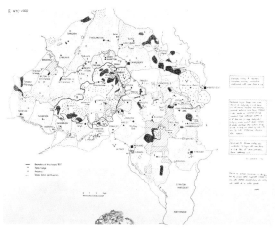

Fig 20: Oxfordshire: sample area 2 - the Wychwood character area (working map by Della Hooke)

of village form), Conservation Area and listed building descriptions (for building material) and the *Register of Parks and Gardens of Special Historic Interest in England* and Davis' map (for deer parks) would be searched and plotted to define the extent of areas which displayed that combination of key characteristics. These data also helped to define any zones of transition between *Historic Landscape Character Areas*. Other sources used included the Geological Survey, the County SMR, Inventory of Ancient Woodland, lists of Sites of Special Scientific Interest (SSSIs) and scheduled monuments, and aerial photographs. Then, within each *Historic Landscape Character Area* early chronological (mainly prehistoric and Roman) depth was documented and the ecological diversity recorded.

In contrast to the attempt to tap into existing expert knowledge, the success of the detailed desk-based analysis was marked. A small number of professionals, within a defined programme and timetable, were able to trawl, analyse and interpret a large number of sources to produce a multi-layered assessment of the extent and character of historic landscape zones within Oxfordshire, without depending on prior assumptions about the landscape.

Table 5: Oxfordshire historic landscape study: criteria used to characterise areas

	Redlands	Limestone belt	Wychwood	Valley landscapes	Corallian ridge	Vale of White Horse and Downs
Topography and soils	★	★	-	★	★	★
Settlement pattern	★	★	★	★	★	★
Size of settlement	★	★	-	-	-	-
Building materials	★	★	-	-	-	★
Nature of enclosure	★	★	-	-	★	-
Ancient woodland	★	★	★	-	-	-
Quarries	-	-	-	★	-	-
Land use	-	-	-	-	★	★
Route ways	-	-	-	-	-	★
Hillforts	-	-	-	-	-	★

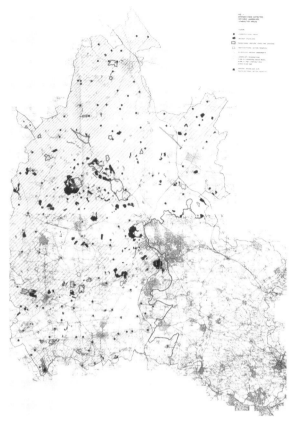

Fig 21: Oxfordshire: sample area 3 - the Vale of the White Horse character area (working map by Della Hooke)

Zoning

Given the constraints of the project methodology and timetable there was a reasonably high level of confidence in the definition of *Historic Landscape Character Areas* and the transitional zones between them. Reference was made to the results of the *top-down* module only when this process had been completed.

The expert judgement (*top-down*) module identified eleven main areas or zones covering the entire study area and a number of sub-zones (twenty-two in all). In contrast the desk-based (*bottom-up*) module identified only six *Historic Landscape Character Areas* covering the study area, although four were further subdivided to produce a total of twelve areas. In both modules of the project the areas identified have been criticised by some for being too topographically controlled. However, a review of the key characteristics for the areas suggest that whilst this may be a justified concern in a small number of the subdivisions proposed by the *bottom-up* module, overall topography and geology is, in this instance, a prime factor in moulding both historic land use and in the survival of greater or lesser elements of former landscape into the current countryside.

Grading and scoring

Despite the deliberate differences of approach, distinct differences in many of the areas identified, and variations in the boundaries between historic landscape zones, there was a surprising degree of consensus in the grading of the historic landscape identified. The *top-down* module saw only one attempt to classify and grade the historic landscape zones and this was based upon a three-tier classification: of national, regional/county, or district/local importance. Only one zone (Wychwood, west of Woodstock) and one sub-zone (Ot Moor near Oxford) were graded as being of national importance, while the scarp and scarp foot of the Berkshire Downs was considered to be close to national status. The remainder of the zones (the vast majority of the study area) was considered to be of at least county importance.

The *bottom-up* module attempted two approaches to grading. The first was simply an impressionistic approach which might be argued to be merely a replication of the expert judgement approach. At the completion of the historic land

Fig 22: Oxford Historic Landscape Character Areas: area 1 and 1A The Redlands; areas 2A and 2B the Limestone Belt; area 3 Wychwood; area 4 valley landscapes; area 5 the Corrallian region; areas 6A and 6B the Vale of the White Horse and the Berkshire Downs

use study Della Hooke graded the areas: two (Wychwood, Figs 20 and 22, zone 3; and the Berkshire Downs/Vale of the White Horse, Fig 22, zone 6A and were given national importance, one (The Redlands, Figs 19 and 22, zone 1) was graded as of regional importance and the remainder as of county importance. In areas of extensive gravel extraction a residual or local interest was scored. As might be anticipated, these were broadly echoed by Paul Chadwick's separate grading, given the predominant role of key characteristics in the methodology. Here Wychwood again scored as being of national importance, Berkshire Downs/Vale as of national/regional importance, Redlands and Ot Moor were thought to be of regional importance, and the remainder of the study area was accorded county importance.

The second approach tried by the *bottom-up* module, applied the Secretary of State's non-statutory criteria (developed for the assessment of ancient monuments) to the key characteristics, time depth and ecological variety as proposed by Lambrick (Lambrick 1992a and b). A 'league table' emerged with 'scores' ranging from 20 to 10. Wychwood scored the highest value and stood clear of the remainder, suggesting that it deserves to be recognised as being of national significance. The remaining scores ran almost sequentially from 14 to 10 suggesting that either the scoring system is not sophisticated enough to distinguish other grades of significance or that the remaining *Historic Landscape Character Areas* are of (virtually) equal significance; probably both suggestions are valid!

Resources

Overall, the *top-down* module required significantly fewer person-hours than the *bottom-up* module, in a ratio of about 1:3. The management and co-ordination of voluntary effort is clearly a very cost-effective approach to historic landscape identification, as long as experts can be convinced to volunteer their input! The cost of commissioning experts formally would be greater, would require significant resources for co-ordination and can be expected to have a longer time-scale attached. However,

without this essential input the *top-down* module would have failed completely in its objectives. (*For a fuller discussion of resourcing implications see chapters 10 and 11*)

Summary

Both modules were able to identify, define and characterise historic landscape within the project study area. Rather than identify representative *historic landscapes*, both modules assessed the whole study area and having characterised the whole, identified a number of *Historic Landscape Character Areas*. The main difference between the modules was that the expert judgement module presented a larger number of (smaller) historic areas, perhaps reflecting subtleties in the landscape which cannot be isolated within the data sources used in the *bottom-up* module. Various rigorous and non-rigorous approaches to grading were tested and a surprising degree of consensus emerged!

As a result, it appears that despite the contrasting methodologies, both have some relevance in any approach to historic landscape identification. Clearly further consideration is required to evolve a methodology which successfully combines *bottom-up* and *top-down* approaches. Our experience suggests that an initial *bottom-up* characterisation of the landscape should precede any approach to experts for their input, and that if their input and assistance is to be forthcoming on any useful scale, the *bottom-up* approach needs to present a reasonably detailed characterisation for the experts to 'tilt at'. (*See also chapters 10 and 11*)

Acknowlegements

The project was carried out by Paul Chadwick in association with Anthony Hitchcott and Della Hooke. The top-down module involved consultations with George Lambrick, and with the conservation officers of Cherwell, Vale of White Horse and West Oxfordshire District Councils. The staff of the Centre for Oxfordshire Studies, including Paul Smith and his colleagues in the SMR, were particularly helpful too.

8: County Durham

Philip Masters

The Durham experimental project was carried out by a team from Chris Blandford Associates and South Eastern Archaeological Services (CBA/SEAS), comprising the author of this chapter and Mark Gardiner, Helen Glass, Julian Munby and Percival Turnbull. It covered a large part of Co Durham defined by the three local authority district council areas of Wear Valley, Durham and Easington, an area of 835 sq km. This area extends from the high Pennine moorland of the upper Wear Valley across the dales landscape of Weardale to the coastal plain characterised by nucleated villages, intensive agriculture, extensive twentieth century development, and the effects of the coal industry (Fig 23). The built up areas of Durham, Crook, Willington, and Bishop Auckland were excluded.

The project's objectives were again those set out in chapter 4. Expert judgement was provided by a *top-down* approach which comprised the canvassing of views, supported by further research. This aspect of the project was directed by the Oxford Archaeological Unit (OAU). The contrasting *bottom-up* approach, consisting of interpretation of the landscape by analysis of

Ordnance Survey maps and field visits, combined with assessment of designations and the County SMR, was carried out jointly by CBA/SEAS. A 'Chinese wall' was maintained between the two aspects of the project and the findings compared at the end. The study began in June 1993 and concluded in October 1993.

Methods

In the *top-down* approach, twenty-six local experts were asked to suggest historic landscape areas in a voluntary context on the basis of their experience and judgement. They were initially invited to identify potential historic landscape areas at 1:100,000 scale. Nine of these experts subsequently attended a seminar at which twenty-one historic landscape areas were identified. OAU then collated these more detailed views and carried out a literature search. Criteria for assessment of these areas (extent, period, themes, main features, relationships, natural landscape, landscape quality) were identified and each was graded as nationally, regionally, or locally important.

Fig 23: County Durham (study area shown in darker tone)

The *bottom-up* approach was undertaken by two experienced archaeologists with limited previous knowledge of the area. In the first phase, historic landscape zones, or more correctly types, were identified from 1:25,000 Ordnance Survey maps on the basis of present-day land use, field and settlement pattern, place-names, vegetation, topography and antiquities (Figs 24 and 25). Subsequent site visits assessed the accuracy of zone boundaries, examined the relationship between the landscape as interpreted from the map and its present visual character. As a consequence it was possible to modify the description of each historic landscape type and its possible evolution. Site visits also provided more detail on the historic features of the landscape. Quantitative methods were not used. This process was largely one of the interpretative application of skills-based professional judgement rather than of the use of existing local knowledge.

The second phase of the *bottom-up* approach began with identifying criteria for assessment which were distinct from, but took account of, those developed for the non-statutory criteria for scheduling (PPG-16) for monuments and sites in the early days of the MPP (Darvill *et al*, 1987) and for landscape areas by Lambrick (1992a and b). They were: scale, setting, rarity, quality, diversity, survival, complementary areas, period diversity, utility, and potential/stability. Using *Historic Landscape Zones* as a basis for interpretation, the study area was surveyed on a systematic basis at the intersection of 5 x 5 km National Grid squares and assessed against these criteria. Scale, setting

and rarity could be evaluated using the map evidence and site appraisal. Quality was inevitably a difficult criterion and depended very much on visual assessment. Diversity was apparent from the map. In contrast, assessment of survival was largely dependent on site inspection, as was the presence of complementary areas and the level of period diversity. Only some aspects of utility such as the frequency of footpaths were apparent and few comments could be made on potential for enhancement.

The thirty 5 x 5 km squares of greatest interest were examined against the assessment criteria and fifteen *Historic Landscape Areas* were identified. Their extent was partly defined by the scale of the landscape, their proximity to complementary areas and high survival of historic landscape elements. Once defined, each *Historic Landscape Areas* was graded as being of high, medium or lesser quality.

As a parallel exercise, the following designated areas or features were plotted at 1:50,000 scale: scheduled monuments, registered historic parks and gardens, National Trust land, ancient woodland, Sites of Special Scientific Interest (SSSI's), Conservation Areas, registered commons, and Areas of Outstanding Natural Beauty (AONB). A visual assessment of the plotting identified nine groupings of designations which related very broadly to *Historic Landscape Areas* and one that did not. In general the correspondence between *Historic Landscape Areas* and areas designated under existing categories of designation was imprecise

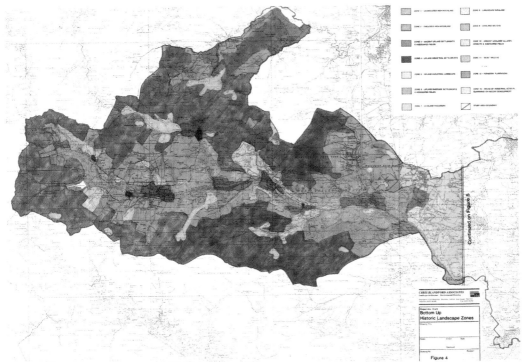

Fig 24 County Durham: historic land-use map of west part of study area (Map by CBA/SEAS)

Information from the County SMR was plotted in 5 x 5 km square units, but was found to offer little help in defining or interpreting *Historic Landscape Areas*. A final, rapid site visit was carried out to refine the *Historic Landscape Areas*, with adjustments being based on poorer or better survival of historic features than was apparent from maps, features of interest just beyond the historic landscape area boundary, and topography.

Results

A comparison of the two approaches showed approximate correspondence between thirteen historic landscape areas, a further eight areas were identified by the *top-down* team alone and two by the *bottom-up* team only. There are four probable reasons for this discrepancy.

- there was no common definition of *historic landscape* and no explicit definition was used by either team

- the *top-down* approach favoured a greater number of landscapes [sic] with prehistoric or with nineteenth and twentieth-century features, reflecting the bias in the experts available and of the visual and map dominance of modern features in much of the landscape

- the *bottom-up* approach attempted to identify as broad a range of historic landscape as possible, including those that were representative of their period or type

- the *bottom-up* approach did not have the site-specific historic and archaeological information which was available to the *top-down* team who tended to put forward a particular place and then locate it within its landscape context

The division of the project into the two approaches was very contrived. In practice, no expert would define the boundaries of an historic landscape area from an armchair and no one using a *bottom-up* approach would ignore the literature or expert advice. Indeed, the general consensus of those involved was that the two methods are aspects of one common expert approach, since in the *bottom-up* method considerable levels of skill are needed in plotting the *Historic Landscape Zones* and identify the *Historic Landscape Areas* . Other studies that have subsequently used a map based approach, such as that for Cornwall (*see annex 2*) have also required such expertise. The mapping of landscape and historic designations and the County SMR proved of limited use in the study. The most helpful designation was Conservation Areas probably because in County Durham they include substantial part of the village hinterland, not just the immediate environment of the buildings. There is scope for the development of a GIS or similar computer-based method to manipulate the Ordnance Survey and other information, and this matter deserves further investigation. However, such a quantitative method would only be of use in identifying historic landscape zones and in identifying potential historic landscape areas. Any classification and grading of historic landscape areas would remain a matter of judgement.

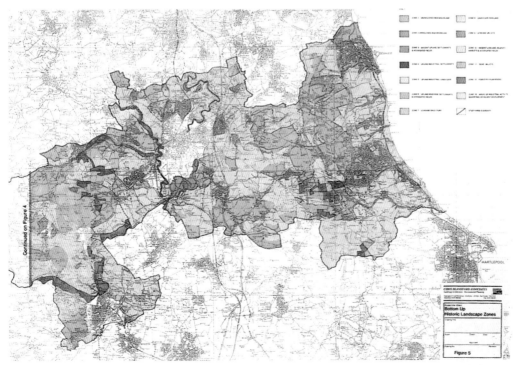

Fig 25 County Durham: historic land-use map of east part of study area (Map by CBA/SEAS)

A composite method incorporating the most useful features of the two approaches was proposed as the primary conclusion of the project. This would begin with expert consultation, a review of the literature recommended by consultees and a site visit for familiarisation. It would be followed by the identification of *Historic Landscape Zones* using a 1:25,000 map base reduced to 1:50,000, defining each *Historic Landscape Type* by a set of key characteristics. Site visits would refine the historic landscape types and characterise them further, using a proforma recording method similar to that used by the Countryside Commission for landscape assessment (Countryside Commission 1993). Using the historic landscape types as a basis, further expert consultation and a literature review, plus an examination of early Ordnance Survey maps and County maps, would sieve out areas of lesser historic interest. The remaining areas would be visited on a systematic basis taking account of the ten assessment criteria identified. Draft *Historic Landscape Areas*, which would take account of territorial and tenurial units such as parishes and estates, would be prepared for expert review, and a final field visit would adjust boundaries.

The *top-down/bottom-up* distinction which the pilot study used has, however, helped to clarify a number of issues that will be of use in future studies. Experts inevitably have a period bias in their knowledge and their view of what is significant, and this seems to have biased the findings of the *top-down* approach. Canvassing of the widest possible range of expert opinion over a longer timescale than was permitted by the pilot study is therefore essential. The areas that they chose, with the exception of Weardale, were often place-focused, and usually settlement-centred, and landscape character was therefore too often defined merely by examining the setting to define the limits of the historic landscape area. This could be turned to advantage if it complements the *bottom-up* approach, but it risks fragmenting the landscape artificially, and undervaluing those areas which exist in the interstice between 'places'. The project also demonstrated that a literature search is of much less use than consultation with experts, who are aware of unpublished work and of both the highlights and the shortcomings of the current literature.

The *bottom-up* method identified the value of the modern 1:25,000 Ordnance Survey map as a basic tool of landscape analysis, combined with a reading of the landscape itself. Its limitations are that very little account can be taken of sub-surface features, but while it shows the pattern of the landscape, in some cases it does not show sufficient specific detail; for instance, in the survey area the map shows the same field pattern was occurring in different areas, but site visits reveal that there were different materials in use for the hedge, wall, or fence boundaries. Nor does it provide information on the relationship of buildings to the surrounding landscape. Apparent historic patterns can be deceptive. For instance, the village of Hunstanworth was assumed to be a medieval village, but the site visit showed it to be an estate village of entirely nineteenth-century origin. The map basis thus has a bias towards more recent features, but equally could not illustrate the complexity of some of them, like for example the nineteenth and twentieth-century mining landscape which is such a feature of this area.

Since knowledge of the historic processes in the study area was not available to the *bottom-up* team, the historic linkages between settlement and the surrounding land, or between uses of different resources at different times, could not be drawn out. As a result, the historic landscape areas defined were representative collections of landscape rather than those necessarily linked by a common history as part of the same estate/parish or similar unit. The availability of expert opinion and, time permitting, analysis of ecclesiastical parish and township boundaries, would remedy this.

Overall, the study went a long way towards meeting the original objectives proposed. Historic landscape types were developed as a means of identifying and characterising the landscape and can be regarded as a neutral and relatively objective method of classification. 'Historic value' for the *bottom-up* method was established by testing the landscape against criteria. Of these, scale, rarity, diversity, complementary areas and period diversity are relatively objective while setting, quality, utility, and potential are more subjective and depend more on the purpose of the classification. In the *top-down* approach a judgement had to be made by an expert about whether an area was significant before it was tested against the defined criteria of extent, period, themes, main features, relationships, natural landscape, and landscape quality, which were less rigorously defined than for the *bottom-up* approach. Both sets of criteria had significant elements of personal judgement which sometimes provided more information about the person making the report than about the area being described: for example 'Tow Law is probably the most depressing place on earth' was one of the more subjective comments perhaps partially redeemed by the qualifying 'probably'.

Both approaches were able to define and grade the areas of interest identified. With more time and research it would probably have been possible to reconcile most of the differences between the two approaches, not least by establishing a rigorous definition of the term *Historic Landscape*. In many cases boundaries could be drawn quite precisely along historic boundaries or abrupt changes in land use.

Finally, the study showed the cost of the two approaches to be broadly similar, but the *bottom-up* approach provided a clear audit trail for *Historic Landscape Types* and *Historic Landscape Areas* which could be refined by further work, and which means both that it is repeatable, and that its results can be tested more easily. However, the combined approach proposed as a result of the study, using a balance of expert opinion, map analysis, examination of selected sources, and fieldwork, would be a more cost effective and accurate approach than either method applied singly, as has been demonstrated subsequently in other parts of the country (*see chapter 11*).

Acknowlegements

The author would like to thank the many people involved in the Durham Historic Landscape Study. Philip Masters of Chris Blandford Associates oversaw the project and provided many useful insights. Mark Gardiner (South Eastern Archaeological Services) and Helen Glass (Chris Blandford Associates) comprised the bottom-up team. The top-down team from the Oxford Archaeological Unit comprised Julian Munby, Dave Wilkinson, and David Miles. Percival Turnbull tied together the detailed results from the seminar of experts. The experts who participated in the top down part of the study were: Dennis Coggins, David Cranstone, Ken Fairless, Ian Forbes, Niall Hammond, Nick Higham, Martin Jones, John Picken, Brian Roberts, Percival Turnbull, Don Wilcock, and Robert Young.

Part III: RESULTS AND CONCLUSIONS

9: Assessment of the pilot projects

Andrew McNab and George Lambrick

The purpose of this chapter is to provide a short critical review of the key issues which are raised by the project before setting out in the next chapter a recommended approach to historic landscape assessment. These issues relate to:

- definitions
- objectives
- approaches
- physical features
- data sources
- data analysis
- characterisation
- evaluation and grading
- scale and levels of study

A brief summary of the questions raised by the project is provided for each of these issues, and conclusions drawn. Reference is made to the earlier pilot study in Kent (*annex 1*) and to the projects own pilot studies: the two pilot studies in Oxfordshire and Durham (*see chapters 7 and 8*), and the two review studies related to farm, parish and estate surveys, andenvironmental assessment (*see chapters 5 and 6*)

Definitions

Discussions of the phrase and concept of *historic landscape* repeatedly arose throughout the project. The term *historic landscape* has gained currency as a shorthand term for describing the historic component of land and landscape but it is not without its critics.

Some prefer the phrase *cultural* landscape to *historic* landscape because it does not appear to exclude prehistoric aspects. It is also a phrase used by ICOMOS in designating World Heritage Sites and increasingly in Council of Europe and European Union documents (for example Council of Europe 1995). However, the term is very all-embracing, involving contemporary as well as past culture, and current attitudes and appreciation as well as material remains of dimension of landscape. It has the additional problem of being equated in some minds with the arts, both of the past but especially current movements and events, rather than with the way social structures have shaped the world.

Landscape is also considered by some to be an unhelpful term because it is too closely associated with visual qualities. 'Landscape' was originally used to describe paintings or pictures of rural scenery and this restricted definition is still promoted in some quarters. The usage of the word has however evolved, and it has come to have a much wider meaning. Thus, amongst archaeologists for example, the concept of sub-surface features forming part of the landscape is widely accepted.

On balance, the already widespread use of the term *Historic Landscape*, and the weaknesses or problems posed by applying the available alternatives, suggests that this is a useful shorthand term for describing the historic dimension of the landscape. None of the objections raised to its use have strength at a practical level.

Objectives

In relation to the pilot studies in Oxfordshire and Durham (*chapters 7 and 8*), the project brief was deliberately vague in specifying objectives for the assessments, requiring methodologies to be tested for a variety of possible end-uses. The authors of the Durham pilot study specifically commented on the difficulty of developing assessment methods without knowing how the results would be used. The review of recent parish, estate, and farm surveys (*chapter 5*) indeed criticised the lack of adequate definition of objectives for such surveys. Similarly, in the environmental assessment review study (*chapter 6*) it was suggested that the objectives of historic landscape assessment were often not stated or difficult to define.

It is axiomatic that the approach to historic landscape assessment will be influenced by the objectives of the assessment and the manner in which the results will be used. Clarity in setting objectives appropriate to the intended purpose of the assessment is therefore critical to success.

Approaches

Most of the historic landscape studies examined in the project (including the Oxfordshire and Durham pilot studies) emphasise academic rather than amenity or management issues. Both the review studies indicated that potential weaknesses may arise from ignoring amenity issues, particularly where public access, the visual setting of important monuments, buildings, or designed landscape is important. The academic approach is likely to be most important for description and understanding of the landscape, but the sort of information needed for conservation and resource management may be not be obtained if a purely academic approach is adopted. The approach adopted should reflect the intended use and the purpose for commissioning the study in the first place.

The Oxfordshire and Durham pilot studies (*chapters 7 and 8*) were intended to test the relative merits of two different approaches based respectively mainly on expert opinion and mainly on data collation and analysis. The conclusion, not surprisingly, is that a sensible approach will combine elements of both expert opinion and data analysis and collation. However, both studies experienced some difficulties in developing the expert opinion approachand it proved not to be as cost-effective as might have been expected. Specific problems related to securing participation, gaining a range of views, and achieving consensus. The first of these problems might be resolved by paying fees to experts consulted, but the general feeling from the pilots was that the end-result would be an inconsistent and highly personalised assessment of landscape character value.

Physical features

The range of historic features comprising *historic landscape* outlined in the English Heritage Consultation Paper (English Heritage 1991d) were used in the pilot studies and appear capable of practical application, though there is scope for some refinement of the categories. The category which has received most critical attention is *historic and natural features*. In the Kent pilot study (*annex 1*) Chadwick found the term imprecise and sought to redefine it as semi-natural habitats, to embrace those natural features which have been most completely influenced by man's management. This suggestion is somewhat clearer than the original, although ecologists and archaeologists would argue that virtually the entire English landscape consists of semi-natural habitats. Chadwick defines the term to include woodland, pasture, commons, watercourses, water meadows, and hay meadows. Essex County Council (1992) have noted the particular importance of wood-pastures, heaths, and deer parks as historic components.

Three broad categories of human interaction with the environment may be distinguished:

- palaeo-environmental deposits such as peat deposits, colluvium, or alluvium, which demonstrate or reflect human impact on the environment but which were not deliberately created

- semi-natural habitats such as woodland or heathland, which demonstrate deliberate human intervention to exploit and maintain specific resources

- man-made features such as ponds, tracks and roads, and hedges

The consideration of the weight which should be attached to subsoil deposits emerged as a significant issue during the project and was highlighted in the earlier pilot study in Kent. There is significant doubt among those specialists concerned with visual and scenic landscape resourcesas to whether subsoil archaeology can be considered part of the landscape. However, in the context of historic landscape assessment, archaeological remains are no less an important part of the physical evidence of landscape development for being invisible. Sub-soil deposits must therefore be considered.

Data sources and investigative techniques

Regional studies

A wide range of data sources were used in the pilot studies as set out in Table 6.

Della Hooke in the Oxfordshire pilot study was one of the few contributors directly to use primary data. The fact that she was only able to sample a third of the selected study area in the time available and that it required fifty-two person-days suggests this is a time-consuming approach. By the nature of such an approach, given that most landscape projects will be time-limited by practical matters such as cost and the need, for example, to feed into local preparation, it is likely that only a selection of sources could be studied in detail, which could bias the study, especially if some key aspects of the character of an area are not reflected in the sources chosen. In addition the use of documentary sources may over-emphasise post-medieval features. It is also apparent that a considerable amount of specialist expertise is needed in their interpretation. The availability and type of documents varies in

Table 6: Data sources for historic landscape assessment at a regional scale

Source	used in Durham study	used in Oxfordshire study	used in Kent study
Primary source			
Tithe awards	-	⋆	-
Estate plans and enclosure maps	-	⋆	-
Early county maps	-	⋆	-
1st Edition OS maps	-	⋆	-
Secondary sources			
Archaeologial and historical lists and designations			
Ancient monuments	⋆	⋆	⋆
SMR	⋆	⋆	⋆
Listed buildings	-	⋆	⋆
Register of Parks and Gardens	⋆	⋆	⋆
Conservation areas	⋆	-	-
Ecological lists and designations			
Site of Special Scientific Interest	⋆	⋆	-
Ancient woodland	⋆	⋆	-
County habitat surveys	-	-	⋆
Landscape lists and designations			
Area of Outstanding Natural Beauty	⋆	-	-
County/local landscape designations	-	-	⋆
Other lists and designations			
Register of commons/village greens	⋆	-	-
National Trust land	⋆	-	-
Other sources			
Air photography	-	⋆	-
Geological survey maps	-	⋆	-
Place names	⋆	-	⋆
Current OS 1:25,000 maps	⋆	-	-

different parts of the country and for different aspects of landscape evolution, with some aspects being totally unrecorded even in historic periods, and great care has to be exercised in their use. The landscape itself, if read archaeologically, can provides a fuller data source. yet it also could lead to misleading conclusions in comparative evaluation. Nevertheless, the use of primary data does provide considerable supporting information which may be effectively mapped.

Secondary data sources, including SMRs and statutory designations such as scheduled monuments, SSSIs, and the *Register of Historic Parks and Gardens* and *Register of Historic Battlefields*, if they are used carefully and in full knowledge of their selective character, can also be helpful. Not surprisingly it is the archaeological and historic data sources which were used most frequently. The *Schedule of Ancient Monuments* and the relevant County SMRs were used in Oxfordshire, Durham and Kent. Neither of the pilot studies found their County SMR data easy to use, and SMR data generally varies greatly in quality and breadth in the records maintained for the different counties.

Listed buildings data was used in the Oxford and Kent analyses. It was not used in Durham because manipulating the abundance of data was not considered cost-effective given the timescale. In truth however, listed buildings data is probably too local and site-orientated to be of much use in landscape scale characterisation, and the same is partly true of SMR point-data and scheduled monuments data. The Durham pilot study included the boundaries of conservation areas. This data source was found valuable although the relatively generous boundaries of conservation areas in Durham, embracing significant rural hinterlands to settlements, is not typical nationally.

Both the Durham and Kent studies used the boundaries of Sites of Special Scientific Interest (SSSIs), the rationale being that SSSIs tend to relate those semi-natural habitats which have been least changed and may therefore be of historic interest. However, the Durham pilot study found that a number of the SSSI designations there related to fairly recent quarries where typical rock exposures were found. This study also revealed a significant duplication between designated Ancient Woodlands and SSSIs. Chris Blandford Associates concluded that, in this case, SSSI data was not particularly relevant to identifying historic landscape. Two studies used the *Inventory of Semi-Natural Ancient Woodland* compiled by English Nature which was found to be a useful source because, although an ecological designation, it has an historical basis in that it records areas of woodland known to have existed prior to 1600.

The Durham pilot study used both the *Register of Common Land* and information on National Trust land ownership. The former was identified both as an historic form of land tenure and as likely to have constrained the pace and scale of change of use. National Trust land was included because of the NT requirement that land held in trust by it must be of natural beauty or historic interest. The boundary of the Area of Outstanding Natural Beauty (AONB) was used in the Durham pilot study but was not found to be particularly useful. County landscape designations however were used as a source of data for identifying historic features in Kent. Other sources included geological survey maps, used in the Oxfordshire pilot study to identify sub-regional areas, place name studies and current 1:25,000 maps. It is worth emphasising that the initial characterisation of historic landscape in Durham was based entirely on the use and interpretation of modern maps.

At the regional scale it appears that it is those data which directly provide either specific information about the nature of the resource (for example ancient woodland), or about its quality (for example scheduled monuments), or preferably both (for example conservation areas and registered parks and gardens) are most useful. SMRs and listed building descriptions contain useful data but it is rarely at landscape-scale, and the number of entries is so great in each case that they cannot easily be used without a process of synthesis. This is only readily achieved where records are computerised. The lesson of the pilot studies appears to be that data should be chosen to suit the particular assessment method and the scale and purpose of that particular assessment, and care must be taken to ensure that such choices are well targeted and cost-effective.

Local studies

Data collection in the five parish, estate, and farm surveys selected for detailed review (*see chapter 5*) reveals a distinctive relationship between the purpose of the surveys and the nature of data collection and field investigation. Those surveys classified by Wessex Archaeology as *Cultural Resource Management Surveys* reveal a distinctive use of field survey techniques: field observations, detailed site survey, hedgerow and boundary surveys and ecological surveys. This fieldwork is in addition to the more conventional use of documentary sources, SMRs etc. By contrast those surveys concerned to inform estate management plans show a much greater reliance on documentary sources and a much lesser use of fieldwork.

The Clouston study of historic landscape assessment as used in Environmental Statements, described in chapter 6, examined in detail five case studies. Each used a wide variety of data sources, normally including both primary and secondary sources. Field investigative techniques were also used in all cases, including geophysical survey, trial trenching, field walking, and ecological surveys.

It is apparent that the smaller the area of historic landscape considered, the more closely do the techniques reflect conventional archaeological survey. Only rarely at the local and site level is there an attempt to identify the patterns or interrelationships which create historic landscape, rather the emphasis was upon individual features. It seems likely that the concept of *historic landscape assessment* is only fully applicable at a sub-regional level, perhaps in local authority terms equivalent to district or county, and that townships/parishes, preferably in groups, are at the lowest practical scale.

Data analysis

In the pilot studies and in most of the local studies reviewed within them, the emphasis was very much on the spatial interrelationship of historic features. Essentially, identified features were mapped and boundaries drawn around them. A very few local studies, most notably the environmental assessment of the Stonehenge proposal, (*see chapter 6*) analysed the data on a chronological basis. This study is particularly noticeable for providing evidence for conjectural reconstructions of areas in the past landscape.

The project revealed very few attempts to integrate assessment of historic features with those of the ecological or scenic qualities of a landscape. The pilot studies and a number of the local studies used ecological data in seeking to identify historic features. However, it was only in the local studies of designed landscape that there was any attempt at a more holistic view of the landscape.

The chronological dimension of historic landscape assessment would seem to merit greater attention, while in the longer term the aim must be to achieve a more integrated approach to landscape assessment.

Characterisation

Both the Oxfordshire and Durham studies attempted to identify areas of consistent historic character; *Historic Landscape Zones* in the terminology recommended below. Again differences between the two studies emerged, particularly the scale of the historic zones identified. The criteria used to characterise sub-regional areas in the Oxfordshire study were geology, soil type, physiography, archaeology and history, settlement patterns, road patterns, historic land use and the present day landscape. The determining factors in each of the areas except Wychwood were topography, geology and soils. The next most important factor was settlement pattern. Other key characteristics were size of settlement, buildings materials, the nature of enclosure and presence or absence of ancient woodland. The characterisation appears to place considerable emphasis on physical factors and the survival of features. Despite the use of primary sources, these played little part in the landscape characterisation, with the possible exception of the period and nature of enclosure. The pattern of areas identified and the key distinguishing characteristics appeared to have similarities with the *New Map Project* of landscape characterisation which was the source of an experimental study in south-west England by the Countryside Commission (Countryside Commission 1994b) leading later to the national *Countryside Character Maps* (Countryside Commission 1998 and Agency 1999).

The Durham experiment identified localised historic landscape zones using a classification based upon a combination of three elements: habitat/land-cover (for example moorland, woodland), function (for example industrial, parkland), and period (for example ancient, recent). The latter reflects Rackham's concept of 'ancient' and 'planned' countryside (Rackham 1986). The characterisation again places emphasis on extant features through its use of existing habitat/land-cover data. Function and period also refer to the dominant function and the dominant period apparent in the present landscape.

The Environmental Statement review in chapter 6 showed that characterisation is still developing in environmental assessments. Methods tend to emphasise the diversity and quality of agglomerations of different types of feature, or the predominant period for which these features represent the most clear, coherent, or interesting pattern. The local landscape survey review (*chapter 5*) commented on the general absence of any process of characterisation in the studies examined.

The variety of criteria used in the Oxfordshire and Durham experiments to characterise the historic landscape represents a considerable advance on traditional approaches which have sought to characterise on the basis of simplistic predominant types (eg enclosure landscape) and have, hence, underestimated the complexity and time depth of the historic landscape. However, it may be argued that the Oxfordshire experiment gave undue prominence to topographic features whilst the Durham study gave undue prominence to extant historic features and tended towards characterising on the basis of predominant features.

The building bricks for characterisation are clearly the individual historic features, and the patterns created by their juxtaposition. Characterisation explores the interrelationship of these features. Traditionally emphasis has been given to agglomerations of features and to predominant features. There is a need to explore the usefulness of other interrelationships such as time, recreating past landscape; or territory, identifying socio-economic divisions in the landscape; or interrelationships of features from different periods.

Evaluation and grading

The Oxfordshire and Durham studies tested no less than six different approaches to evaluation and grading. Two sets of issues arose relating to the areas to be evaluated, and a separate set of issues related to the criteria to be used. If evaluation is to be used, should it be applied to the whole of the landscape, and should all the landscape be graded as to its historic importance? Such an approach is in keeping with the holistic approach to landscape conservation. Alternatively should individual areas of importance be identified? Such an approach is in keeping with the traditional identification of only the finest landscapes or buildings. The pilot studies developed techniques for both approaches.

The second issue relates to the areas which are to be evaluated. In the Oxfordshire pilot study evaluations were made of the *Historic Landscape Zones*. Such an approach parallels the developing methodology of visual landscape assessment, where characterisation is seen as an essential prelude to evaluation. By contrast, in the Durham pilot study, areas of historic landscape importance were identified quite separately from historic landscape zones. The most common approaches were expert opinion and the Secretary of State's criteria for assessing scheduled monuments. Only the Durham pilot study offered any significant modification, emphasising amenity issues such as scale, setting, quality and utility; and functional issues, principally complementary areas.

The *top-down* and *bottom-up* approaches to evaluation and the different results they produced offer some useful insights. In Durham, the different approaches identified the same basic areas as *Historic Landscape Zones*. It was felt that in many cases more detailed consideration would resolve such differences as had arisen. However, this study was also of interest in suggesting that the definition of *Historic Landscape Zones* was easier in the less well preserved lowlands (where landscape of special historic interest are more likely to stand out) than in the uplands which are generally seen as being of high quality across their whole extent. For the uplands, the approaches tended to diverge, the experts suggested that it might be appropriate to define key components worthy of conservation rather than defining entire areas, while the data analysis team effectively suggested the selection of representative sample areas (although these were large areas, in one case a complete parish).

The local study review (*chapter 5*) and, to some extent, the Environmental Statement review (*chapter 6*) demonstrated the better established application of evaluation and grading for individual elements within the landscape. In the case of the Weld Estate case study, (*see chapter 5*) this was based on management priorities rather than intrinsic qualities which is the more normal approach. The A27 and the Oxford Flood Plain cases (*see chapter 6*) suggested ways of grading the historic interest of the whole of the landscape based on the diversity, value, and coherence of historic landscape components. Most of the studies which attempted grading used three or four simple grades related to quality or level of interest (national, county, local, absent).

The debate about approaches to evaluation and grading will probably not be productive until techniques of analysis and characterisation are more advanced, and unless there is a specific reason for a particular evaluation such as need to make a selection of potential development sites, but even for these purposes the better approach may be to undertake the identification of historic landscape zones appropriate to specific types of land use or development. In other words the specific objectives of any particular study may well suggest the most appropriate techniques.

Scale and levels of study

The regional pilot studies analysed historic landscape at a variety of scales:

- by 1km grid square in the Kent study

- by something approaching a field by field basis in the Durham study

- by parish in the first part of Oxfordshire pilot study

- by local areas as in the *top-down* approach in Durham

- by broad sub-regions as in the second stage of the Oxfordshire project

No guidance was provided as to the appropriate scale of analysis and the broad conclusion would seem to be that the historic interest of landscape can be identified at a variety of scales. For most purposes, especially where the primary aim is to recognise and appreciate broad patterns and process, scales that allow large areas to be characterised are to be preferred, and it is this scale which English Heritage supported projects have focused on subsequently (*see chapter 11*). It is however for potential users of the assessment to specify which scale would be most appropriate.

Chapter 10: Conclusions and recommendations

Andrew McNab and George Lambrick

This chapter sets out to describe and define *Historic Landscape Assessment*, its principles, objectives and uses. It recommends a terminology and an approach to assessment. The chapter draws mainly on the research project described in Part II and the analysis of their results in chapter 9, but also on discussions with the project's steering group, between project members, and at a number of seminars organised by English Heritage during the project. Since it was first set out, the approach has been used elsewhere with success, notably the first county-wide project in Cornwall (*annex 2*) and subsequently in several other counties, as described in chapter 11. It therefore constitutes the framework for English Heritage's preferred approach to historic landscape assessment and conservation.

Principles

Historic Landscape Assessment (or characterisation) is concerned with understanding and explaining the physical evidence at landscape scale in the present day environment of past human activity and organisation. It looks at the interrelationships between human society and the environment through time, with specific focus on the historic landscape character of the current environment.

In Britain, the landscape has everywhere been exploited by man and it has, in its modified as well as 'natural' form, in turn profoundly affected the nature of this exploitation. All landscape has an historic dimension. What varies from area to area is the process of change, the resultant survival of physical remains, the degree of their surviving integrity and diversity, and the interpretation and perceived quality of such evidence.

Historic Landscape Assessment needs to be considered in the context of other characterisation and assessment techniques. The Countryside Commission's recommended approach to landscape assessment is principally concerned with the visual qualities of landscape although with some consideration of historic and cultural issues. Recently the Commission has prepared guidance on the historic component of landscape assessment its publication *Views from the past* (Countryside Commission 1994a, 1996). Attempts have also been made to integrate historic features more closely into landscape assessment undertaken by other bodies. The

identification of natural areas by English Nature is primarily concerned with the ecological qualities of the landscape but has also proved a good framework for explaining the historic origins of ecological patterns and, in due course, for the application of *Historic Landscape Assessment*. The Natural and Countryside Character Areas defined by English Nature and the Countryside Commission in many cases have boundaries or characters delimited as much by cultural as natural factors.

While comprehensive and holistic views of landscape are highly important, there is also however a need for an assessment process concerned specifically with the historic dimension of landscape. This should ideally take account of the full range of past interrelationships between people, and between people and their environment, and should reflect the full depth of how those interrelationships have changed through time and space. Taking account of the time dimension potentially makes *Historic Landscape Assessment* more complex than its visual and ecological counterparts.

Physical evidence relevant to *Historic Landscape Assessment* comprises palaeo-environmental deposits, man-made archaeological remains, buildings and structures, landscape features such as field boundaries and ponds, and semi-natural features such as heathland, woodland, and grassland. These elements need to be identified and their interrelationship analysed as part of *Historic Landscape Assessment*. Such analysis is a largely interpretative process of characterisation. In this process individual elements come to be seen as 'components' of a wider system, which has its own character and value. Judgements of relative value in *Historic Landscape Assessment* can be made about individual components, types of components, and about the historic landscape types as defined by or derived from an analysis of the interrelationships of elements. It is not recommended that judgements should be made on the relative value of topographically or spatially defined samples of the landscape.

The detailed methodology adopted by any *Historic Landscape Assessment* must be tied to clearly defined objectives in terms for example of research or practical policy making, future management, or particular development proposals.

Objectives

The objectives of any *Historic Landscape Assessment* and characterisation are likely to include all, or at least many, of the following:

- to promote an awareness of local identity and regional diversity

- to recognise such past social, economic, political, and cultural interactions through time between people and the environment, as revealed by the surviving landscape

- to promote the understanding, appreciation, and conservation of the physical evidence (both archaeological and natural) for the development of human society within the landscape

- to identify, describe, characterise, and evaluate the historic dimension of areas of landscape to facilitate conservation policies and practice

- to promote an appreciation and understanding of the landscape context of individual historic and archaeological sites

Definitions and terminology

Historic landscape: this is a term already in widespread use. When used carefully, it has some value as a shorthand descriptive term for the historic dimension of the whole landscape, for that part of the environment's character which derives from an appreciation and understanding of its past. The term cannot be sensibly used however to denote a discrete area within the landscape.

Historic landscape character: is defined by analysing the interrelationship of historic landscape features and identifying patterns. Areas that are so identified may be termed historic landscape types. These types will form a patchwork, or mosaic, within a larger area, such as a character area.

***Historic Landscape Assessment* (or Characterisation)**: is thus a reasonable description of the process of interpreting the historic and archaeological interest of an area of land. In parallel with the terminology used by the Countryside Commission, *Historic Landscape Assessment* should be taken as having a specific meaning intended to embrace the entire process by which the historic dimension of the landscape is identified, described, characterised, and if appropriate evaluated.

The individual archaeological remains, buildings and structures, landscape features, semi-natural habitats and palaeo-environmental deposits which contribute to *Historic Landscape Character* within a specific area may best be referred to as *Historic Landscape Features*. Where their interrelationship is significant in defining *Historic Landscape Character*, they will be seen as contributory elements within a specific context, and may be referred to as *Historic Landscape Components*.

Where an area is evaluated and is recognised as important, it may be termed an *Area of Particular Historic Landscape Interest*. This might be qualified according to the degree of importance. At national level for example, one might refer to *Areas of Special Historic Landscape Interest* and at a local level to *Areas of Local Historic Landscape Interest*. Any such usages need to be wary however of belittling the historic character of other areas of landscape. In most cases, they will have a limited area of application (for example to target agri-environment funding schemes).

Reference to an *historic landscape*, as applied to a specific place, should strictly be used only to mean an interpretative model of what a particular area of land may have been like at particular periods in the past.

Uses

Historic landscape assessment is needed:

- to promote understanding and enjoyment of the landscape

- to inform Development Plans, decisions on planning applications and land-management practices

- to aid the design of development proposals (through environmental assessment)

Historic Landscape Assessment therefore may need to be carried out at a variety of scales from the local to the regional/national, although at very local scales levels approach the site-specific for which these assessment approaches are unlikely to be useful. Any *Historic Landscape Assessment* should also aim to serve the interests and needs of a variety of types of user including the needs of for example, the general public, landowners, countryside managers, and planners.

A recommended approach to Historic Landscape Characterisation

Set out below is a general approach which is intended to be capable of application at a variety of scales, by a variety of users, for a variety of purposes. Some suggestions are made about the most appropriate methodology for different purposes. It has already been used very successfully in Cornwall, Derbyshire, and subsequently at a number of other places (Chapter 11, Fairclough 1999c). The general approach can now be assumed to have been validated.

The recommended approach has five main components:
Study objectives
Data collection
Data analysis and characterisation
Evaluation and grading
Policy implications and recommendations

For relatively straightforward studies these could be seen as a simple series of sequential tasks, and some may be carried out simultaneously. For large or complex studies the tasks may need to be carried out in an iterative manner. This particularly applies to the identification of historic landscape features and to the process of characterisation. As the depth of understanding of an area increases, so there will be a need to reconsider, review and adjust other elements to ensure that the study is still well-focused on its original objectives.

Study objectives

The first stage of any historic landscape assessment should be to assess the scope of the study. This will involve producing a statement defining:

- the objectives of the study and the likely use of the results (for example developing awareness of local identity, academic understanding, designations and planning policies, development appraisal, management or grant assessment

- the scale of the area to be assessed and, if appropriate, definition of *core* and *peripheral* areas

- the types of information required both in relation to the historic environment and the objectives of the study

- the levels of information and analysis required to achieve the study objectives

It will also be useful to prepare a method statement identifying:

- the main topographical, historic, archaeological and other types of evidence, and potential sources and techniques for data gathering

- the approach to and criteria for characterisation

- the need and criteria for evaluation

- the approach to formulating action following the assessment

Data collection

A basic description of the study area is needed at an early stage in any study in order to ensure that more detailed information gathering and interpretation is well focused on relevant issues. Such background analysis could include:

- geology

- landform

- hydrology and drainage

- climate

- environmental evidence

- archaeology

- history

- vegetation cover

- current and recent land use trends

A key element of any *Historic Landscape Characterisation* is the identification and description of individual *Historic Landscape Features* and their interrelationships, and of the sequence of historic land use in an area. Data sources used to identify historic features will vary according to the scale of the study and the resources available. Chapter 9 contains a review of data sources used in the pilot projects and their comparative usefulness. The objective of this stage of the process is to identify sufficient historic features to enable characterisation. These will included features both above and below ground, their nature, function, origin, survival, and distribution.

Data analysis and characterisation

The key to understanding historic landscape lies in analysing and interrelating the individual historic features. Three such analyses have traditionally been used. First, features have been mapped in order to identify their relative density, thus identifying concentrations of features worthy of conservation. Secondly, areas have been characterised on the basis of the predominance of components or systems of a particular age, such as '*enclosure landscape*', although this analysis should not completely overlook other aspects of the landscape of different date or type, particularly with a view to recognising time-depth; issues of survival and preservation become problematic in such an approach. Thirdly, features of a similar age have been mapped thus producing landscape maps for different periods.

There is a need for a more profound analysis of the functional, spatial, and temporal relationships between historic features to establish how they relate to each other as components of wider socio-economic systems, and how they relate to the natural environment. This is likely to be facilitated by early consultation with local experts. Suggested criteria for such analyses are:

- predominant and subordinate periods represented by historic features in the landscape

- predominant socio-economic themes and functions represented

- typical components reflecting themes and functions

- patterns of temporal relationships, notably sequences of continuity or change

- patterns of spatial relationships

- relationships with the natural environment

Interrelationships may be explored and presented using:

- previous studies

- mapping techniques (for example sieve/overlay maps)

- geographical analyses (for example of settlement pattern and transport systems, social and economic organisation)

- historic analyses (for example of political context, estate history)

- archaeological analyses (for example of spatial and temporal relationships, dating, typologies)

- computer analysis (for example multi-variate analysis, GIS and CAD)

- matrix analyses (*see Table 7 for an example*)

The objective of this stage of characterisation is to identify the most significant interrelationships between historic features and to subdivide the study area into areas of different historic character, or *Historic Landscape Zones*. These areas are likely to be characterised as much by their heterogeneous as their homogenous character, as in, for example, the *Countryside Character Map* (Countryside Commission 1998 and Agency 1999), and the settlement mapping work carried out for the MPP (Roberts and Wrathmell, 1995 and forthcoming).

Evaluation and grading

Whereas characterisation is intended to increase understanding, evaluation is concerned with comparing the relative values of different areas, more particularly where there are differing aspects of character. Evaluation is inevitably difficult and may not be necessary for many purposes if types or areas have been fully characterised. It may be counter-productive if it encourages devaluation of surrounding areas. Evaluation, like environmental impact assessment or evaluation within the PPG-16 framework, needs to be measured against a particular need; global, once and for all, evaluation is rarely justified at landscape-scale in particular. The next few paragraphs give advice on appropriate criteria for evaluation in cases where it is thought necessary to go beyond characterisation for the purposes of formulating advice, policy, or decision-making.

The Secretary of State's criteria for the evaluation of monuments recomended for scheduling as extended by the MPP can be used to produce a simplified threefold grouping of criteria, applicable both to historic landscape components and zones:

Academic/scientific: rarity; survival and potential; period; documentation; scale; group value; diversity and integrity of evidence; non-historic conservation/scientific value.

Table 7 : Example of chronology versus process matrix analysis (Oxfordshire)

Historic Landscape Character		Pleistocene	Earlier Prehist			Later Prehist	Romano-British	Earlier Medieval		Later and post Medieval		Industrial	
Themes	Functions	Lower Mid Pal	Upper Pal/ Mes	Early mid Neo	LNE EBA	LBA IA	RB	Migr	Early Med	Late Med	Post Med	Ind	Mod
Impact on environment	Clearance				■■■	■■■	■■■	■■■	■■■				
	Soil erosion				■■■	■■■	■■■	■■■	■■■	■■■	■■■	■■■	■■■
Subsistence and resource exploitation	Hunting/gathering	?	?	?									
	Arable land use								■■■	■■■			
	Pastoral land use			?	■■■	■■■	■■■	■■■	■■■	■■■	■■■	■■■	■■■
	Woods/forestry						?	?	■■■	■■■	■■■	■■■	■■■
	Water resource				——	——	——	——	——	——	——	——	——
	Wetland resource												
	Field patterns					——	——		——	——	——	——	——
Industry and crafts	Extractive industry									?	——	——	
	Processing industry									——	——	——	
	Power/technology									——	——	——	
	Rural crafts					?	?	?					
Trade and exchange	Transport								——	——	——	——	——
	Commerce								——	——	——	——	——
Landholding and land allotment	Transhumance							?	?				
	Tenure								■■■	■■■	■■■	■■■	■■■
	Intercommoning								■■■	■■■	■■■	■■■	■■■
	Estates								——	——	——	——	——
Community and population	Settlement pattern		?	?	■■■	■■■	■■■	■■■	■■■	■■■	■■■	■■■	■■■
	Settlement density								——	——	——	——	
	Social hierarchy				■■■	■■■	■■■	■■■	■■■	■■■	■■■	■■■	■■■
	Utilities										——	——	——
	Political/administrative								——	——	——	——	——
	Military							■■■	■■■	■■■	■■■	■■■	
	Territory					?		——	——				
Ideology	Funerary		?		■■■			——	——	——	——	——	——
	Worship			?		?		■■■	■■■	■■■	■■■	■■■	■■■
	Ceremonial			?									
	Commemorative												
Social and aesthetic	Recreation									■■■	■■■	■■■	
	Sport									——	——	——	
	Landscape design										■■■	■■■	
	Architectural design									■■■	■■■	■■■	■■■

■■■ = key interest　　—— = secondary interest

abbreviations:
Lower Mid Pal; Lower Middle Palaeolithic; Upper Pal/ Mes: Upper Palaeolithic/Mesolithic; Early to mid Neo: Early to mid Neolithic; LNE EBA: Late Neolithic/early Bronze Age; LBA IA: Late Bronze Age/Iron Age; RB: Romano-British; Migr: Migration period; Early Med: Early medieval; Late Med: Late medieval; Post Med: Post-medieval; Ind: Industrial; Mod: Modern

Characterisation matrix

The idea of this technique is to act as a checklist rather than as the characterisation as such, and it is intended as no more than a shorthand means of deriving a very crude visual and easily assimilated pattern from complex issues that are likely to deserve more detailed examination and assessment. As such its value is as a trigger to ensure consideration of all available issues more than as a stand-alone analytical tool. Nevertheless it may prove capable of demonstrating time-depth or recurrence of particular themes and functions, or the variety of themes and functions present at any particular period. Annotating matrix boxes with simple value judgements makes it possible to judge the overall variety and time-depth represented within an area. It may also highlight main conservation issues, including those cases where it is not the diversity of interest that matters but the overriding value of a particular area or component representing a single theme at a particular period. The example shown is briefly defined in the top-down Oxfordshire study as a sub-zone (K1) which comprises the historic core of the city of Oxford and its northern expansion, the Port Meadow grazing lands, and the woods, parkland and village of Wythern.

The technique has since been used elsewhere, notably in Cornwall (Herring 1998, figs 31–3) and the Isle of Axholme (Miller 1999c, Figs 21–2)

Amenity: access; scale; quality of setting; visual character; diversity and interest of intrinsic character.

Management/future development: survival and potential; vulnerability; conservation value; access; key visual and physical characteristics; group value, economic viability; trajectory of change.

It is crucial to keep in mind the full range of values applicable (see English Heritage 1997a, 4).

Each of these criteria can be regarded as of high, medium, or low value. The grouping of these criteria has the advantage of being fairly easily used for rapid assessment of numerous landscape components or small zones, where the number of elements to be evaluated may make it impractical to undertake detailed explanation of each criterion for all of them. These three broad criteria may be used in a variety of ways according to the objectives and scale of study. Their relative weighting may be varied to meet the objectives of the particular study, and it may well be appropriate in some cases to treat them summarily as three basic criteria forestablishing action priorities.

Grading may be applied to individual historic features or components or to historic landscape zones or areas of historic landscape interest. Areas of historic landscape interest may embrace parts or all of different historic landscape zones. A grading system which identified levels of interest (ie national, regional, local and potential) might fit well with existing systems, but in general terms it will be preferable to regard the historic landscape as a major aspect of environmental capital, without necessarily imposing a hierarchy of grading. Its characteristics provide a framework for helping to make sustainable decisions (*see* English Heritage 1997a, *and chapter 11*).

Policy implications and recommendations

This stage will involve relating the information about historic landscape and the increased understanding of its character to the study objectives. This might include consideration of general implications such as the nature of land use change and policy requirements, the potential effects of designation procedures, management options, presentation options, land use trends, development threats, types of impact arising from proposed developments and any other relevant factors. At a more specific level it will involve the analysis of actual effects, opportunities, risks, and appropriate policies.

General recommendations will outline the basic requirements to achieve the objectives of the study. These could be to confirm a need for designation, define the direction of agri-environmental policies, devise planning policies with or without some form of designation or draw up local development plans. They could include explaining the need for a management plan, the justification for a specific presentation package, the need for criteria against which to judge development proposals, or the need for mitigation of a new development.

More specific recommendations will describe the way in which the objectives of the study can be met by specific actions. These could be suggested boundaries for designation, draft policy statements, draft or synopsis of management plan, draft criteria for agricultural incentives or cross-compliance, outline presentation proposals, or specific mitigation measures for development.

Early use of the approach

Since 1993–4, the approach which emerged from the research project described in this book has been tested in a number of ways. Foremost among these is a broad-brush approach to assessment based on historic land use. This was pioneered in Cornwall and has since been carried out over several other large areas : the former county of Avon, the Cotswolds AONB, the Peak National Park and Hampshire. Work is also underway in Nottinghamshire, Derbyshire and Suffolk, and is being planned for Lancashire and Gloucestershire. This work is described further in the next chapter.

11: Historic landscape and the future

Graham Fairclough

The preceding chapters have summarised the *Historic Landscape Project*, and its conclusions, notably that the most appropriate approach to the understanding, conservation, and managed evolution of the historic landscape is through the use of assessment and characterisation techniques to inform an understanding of requirements for change and management. The method proposed is centred on the idea of a broad characterisation of the landscape's historic dimension within large scale heterogenous areas which allow broad patterns of historic landscape to be discerned.

The work carried out during the project covered a wide range of ideas and methods. None of the experimental projects described in Part II on their own provide a complete solution to all historic landscape work. They do however offer examples of approaches that can be modified or adapted, or used in combination with other techniques. More recent work by English Heritage and local authorities has built on the overall approach developed by the project, and advocated in chapter 10. This ongoing work has taken some techniques from both the Durham and Oxford studies, described in chapters 7 and 8, but developed them in new directions. Several projects have been carried out in areas as diverse as Cornwall, the Peak National Park and Hampshire, and these now represent the most advanced method of historic landscape assessment at a county scale. This chapter will summarise some of this recent work, and then draw final conclusions on the way ahead.

The progress which has been made in England since the *Historic Landscape Project*, starting with the Cornwall method pioneered in 1994–5, has taken two forms: first, application of the method to other areas at a similar, largely county, level and second, the further development, modification and 'proving' of the technique. In the latter category, the main areas

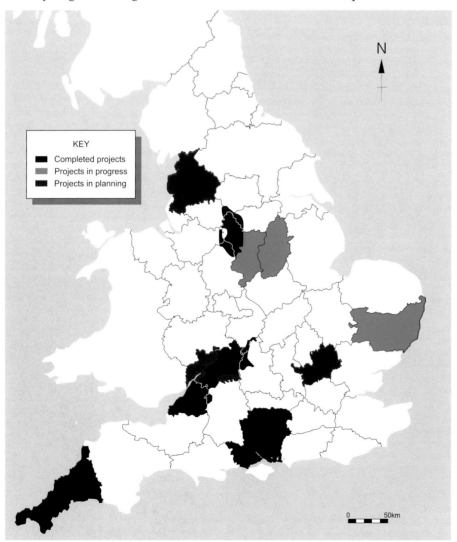

Fig 26: Historic landscape characterisation EH/LA projects at the end of 1998

of development have been the increasing use of GIS applications and techniques, and experiments with use of historic maps, hand in hand with more sophisticated and flexible typologies of historic land-use types, and correlation with (or historic analysis of) other landscape work, for example the Countryside Commission's Countryside Character Areas.

The current position with this programme of work in England is shown on Fig 26. Historic landscape character maps were complete by the end of 1998 for Cornwall, Avon (ie the former, 1974, county that was abolished in 1996), the Derbyshire part of the Peak National Park, the Cotswolds AONB and Hampshire. In progress at that date were historic landscape characterisation in two other counties (Derbyshire outside the Peak and Nottinghamshire) and a large sub-regional area of East Anglia, commencing with Suffolk and Hertfordshire (see also Fairclough 1999b and 1999c).

Cornwall

The Cornwall historic landscape assessment was the first of these projects, and pioneered many of the detailed techniques that have been used and developed in later projects. It was carried out in 1994–5 for the Countryside Commission and English Heritage with district council support by

the Cornwall Archaeological Unit (CAU) of Cornwall County Council, in association with Landscape Design Associates, (LDA and CAU 1994). It grew directly out of an earlier smaller project covering only Bodmin carried out by CAU with Land Use Consultants for the Countryside Commission with English Heritage (Countryside Commission 1994c, 1994d).

The Cornwall projects had three main origins. First, they grew out of several years work and experience by Cornwall Archaeological Unit in developing landscape-scale approaches to the historic environment of the county. The CAU had thus laid much of the necessary groundwork for this type of broad-brush method of historic and archaeological landscape characterisation (Johnson 1998). A second genesis came from the ideas emerging from the English Heritage research project that has been described in chapters 7 and 8 of Part II above. The two regional studies, notably that in County Durham, were particularly helpful, as were the discussions which helped to define some of the general theoretical points summarised in Part I. Finally, their third point of origin lay in the ideas about historic landscape character and process that were formulated in *Views from the past* (Countryside Commission 1994a), for which the two Cornwall projects were seen as a testing ground.

An account of the Cornwall project is

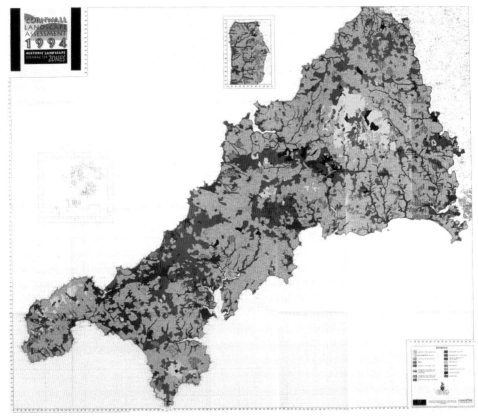

Fig 27: Cornwall: historic landscape character map (1994) as published in Cornwall Landscape Assessment (Cornwall County Council 1996)

presented in annex 2, since it is a pioneering project. Peter Herring describes in some detail how the project was defined and carried out, and how its results are already being widely used by CAU for conservation, research, and development control. There is no doubt that this approach to the historic landscape's characterisation is viable and cost-effective and demonstrably of use in the real world of conservation, planning and land-management decision-making. A draft method statement was produced at the time (Landscape Design Associates and Cornwall Archaeological Unit 1995), and a more formal report has since been published in (Herring 1998).

Since completion, the Cornwall map has proved invaluable in a variety of spheres. It now routinely provides an interpretative backdrop for SMR data and its use in development control. It has provided a hitherto missing framework for larger scale, more local, work on the landscape. Such more detailed work in its turn has both refined and confirmed the broad conclusions reached by the whole county characterisation project. This ability is one of the map's main benefits, and one of the clearest demonstrations of the effectiveness of broad-brush characterisation. The map also gives a basis for defining agri-environmental and other conservation priorities for the historic landscape in Cornwall, facilitating dialogue between archaeologists, ecologists, and planners, and strengthening public understanding of the landscape's historic character in the first place. This latter point is particularly important when compared with the devaluing effect in public consciousness of selective designation. Concentration on the character of the whole landscape rather than special parts allows due recognition of all its components and attributes, which in turn allows the everyday and the 'everywhere' to move centre stage. In Cornwall, this move has played a significant role already in the recent growth of a stronger sense of identity rooted in Cornwall's distinctive historic environment (Johnson 1998, and Herring and Johnson 1999). It leads, for example, to a wider recognition (and the demonstration through landscape characterisation) of the great antiquity and time-depth of the Cornish agricultural landscape and its settlement patterns. It also creates the climate for developing a better appreciation of the slightly more recent (though still several centuries old) influence of mining activity on all aspects of much of the Cornish landscape.

Cornwall, therefore, has provided the first very successful use of historic landscape

characterisation at county scale, and has thus validated the approach outlined here as a result of the English Heritage historic landscape project. The uses to which the Cornwall historic landscape map is already being applied include all the targets for uses and users that were defined at the start of the English Heritage project (*see chapter 4*), and are starting to provide case studies of how characterisation leads directly to conservation and planning decisions. It also demonstrates conclusively that such an approach, enthusiastically embracing wherever possible the local and the commonplace and referring to everyone's locality as well as to special places, offers the rewards of greatly enlarged public awareness and support for the continued conservation and management of the historic landscape.

Other projects since Cornwall

This is not the place for detailed descriptions of all the other projects which have been carried out by local authorities with English Heritage to implement of the conclusions of the *Historic Landscape Project*. Each will in time produce their own reports. It may be helpful however to make a few comments on the various developments of the original Cornwall methodology which later projects have explored. Although very successful, the Cornwall approach should not yet be taken as the last word in methodology. All later projects have borrowed heavily from the Cornwall method (as set out in the interim method statement, Landscape Design Associates and Cornwall Archaeological Unit 1994) and in this way they have further confirmed its overall effectiveness, practicality and uses. They have also altered it however, by learning from each other, and adapting the basic method to different local situations. The methodology has therefore, since the completion of the project, been continually evolving.

Where necessary, each project has tailored the method to local circumstances, both in terms of regional and local landscape diversity and in terms of the particular requirements of local authorities and communities at different stages of development reflecting the pace and direction of change in their economies. Nor has it been the aim to produce a standardised map of landscape character throughout all of England. The rich local and geographical diversity of the country's historic landscape deserves more attention than that (see Fairclough 1999b, 1999c and 1999d and forthcoming, and Herring and Johnson 1999).

Avon: this project was almost entirely funded by the old county council. It proceeded parish by parish, which allowed local experts to contribute their considerable understanding of the landscape within the overarching framework of the strategic methodology. During the Avon project, the typology used in Cornwall was modified to suit local needs, for example by adding new types to reflect the Avon Levels, while greater attention was given to variations in the character of post-medieval enclosure and to land use immediately pre-dating enclosure, an aspect developed further in the Cotswolds project currently underway. Another benefit of the Avon project was that it was carried out to the boundaries of the 1974 county of Avon immediately before its abolition and replacement by four separate unitary authorities; the value of the map is therefore enhanced by providing a regional context to decisions within the new smaller authorities. The Avon map was digitised as a second stage of the project which allowed the data to be manipulated and rearranged in different patterns, and against varying backdrops.

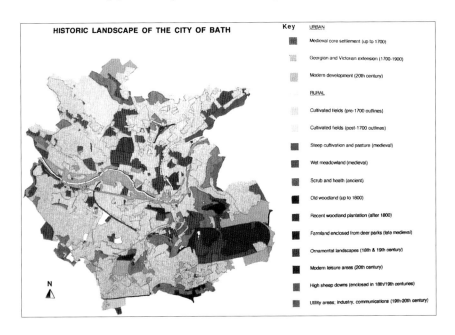

Fig 28: Avon: extract of historic landscape characterisation map showing Bath city, Bath and North East Somerset (by Mike Chapman for Avon County Council)

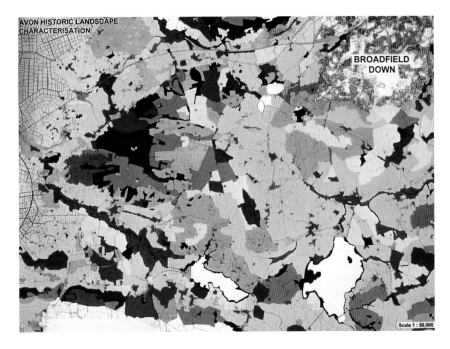

Fig 29: Avon: extract of historic landscape characterisation map showing area around Broadfield, South Gloucestershire (by Mike Chapman for Avon County Council)

The Cotswold project: since it took as its boundary that of one of the larger AONBs (for a discussion of historic landscape in AONBs, see Coupe and Fairclough 1991; for a landscape assessment of the Cotswolds AONB, see Countryside Commission 1990) also broke new ground in covering parts of several counties. Its main innovation however was in mapping directly onto GIS rather than digitising as a second stage. Later projects (for example Hampshire) have followed this experience, and the future aim will be for projects to map onto GIS directly. The main immediate result of greater use of GIS in the Cotswolds has been the recognition that the stage of simplifying the Historic Landscape Assessment types map into a zones map which the Cornwall project carried out (*see annex 2*) is not necessary as a once-and-for-all exercise if GIS is utilised. Instead, simplified zone maps can be produced relatively rapidly whenever required, and (most importantly) for a variety of purposes. Types can be amalgamated to answer specific queries (for example the distribution, location, and relative significance of meadow and grassland), and either simplified or extrapolated to produce, for example, late medieval land use reconstructions. In addition, the maps could in future be simplified in scale and detail to become part of a composite map covering larger areas at regional or perhaps even national scales.

Furthermore, the corollary of this ability is that it is feasible to work with more complex and sophisticated classifications (if these are warranted) without fear of attendant data-handling problems. The Cotswolds classification, for example, developed a hierarchical structure: one level denoting current land-use type (for example eighteenth-century parliamentary enclosure), a second level denoting (where 'known') the preceding land use (for example open fields, common grazing) and a third (rarely used) level denoting more local characteristics. GIS mapping allows these finer distinctions to be displayed, or ignored; if displayed, they can be analysed at any one of a number of levels. Reconstruction of a specific aspect of the landscape, for example the extent of open fields in the fourteenth century, thus becomes a realistic prospect. Work in Hampshire took this further, successfully using up to 80 different types without losing sight of the overall pattern of the landscape at county scale.

The Peak National Park: here the historic landscape characterisation map attempted a closer exploration of time-depth. Reconstructions of past landscape although speculative, are useful in providing some generalised depth to the all important 'current' historic land-use map. This aim lay behind experiments in the Peak Project to produce period maps as well as '1990s' maps. The

Fig 30: Cotswolds AONB: part of the historic landscape characterisation map (by Jon Hoyle for Gloucestershire County Council)

Peak Project had twin origins: to build on Cornwall's experience, but also to contribute to EH's Monuments Protection Programme (MPP) research on the landscape context of Derbyshire's lead-mining industry, in particular how the relationship of mining with agriculture has affected the visible landscape. For this latter aim a stronger emphasis on chronology was needed. The process of mapping past landscape was facilitated by the existence of substantial collections of historic estate maps in the archives of Chatsworth and Haddon. These have allowed 'time-slices' to be produced for *c*1650, 1750, 1800, and 1850 as well as *c*1995. These period maps are of course not complete, and 'white areas' (ie gaps in historic coverage) increase the further back the series extends, but it is proving possible to fill in the gaps by extrapolation from map to map, aided too by the better understanding of the landscape history of the area which the project has generated.

It is too early to say much about the other projects underway shown on Fig 26. The benefit of complete *Historic Landscape Characterisation* maps for a region as large as Derbyshire, Nottinghamshire, Avon, and the Cotswolds, (if Warwickshire could be included to fill the gap) scarcely needs stating. In addition, each project to date has also brought in new ideas and the methodology is continually advancing. Of the two most recent projects, Hampshire was the first to

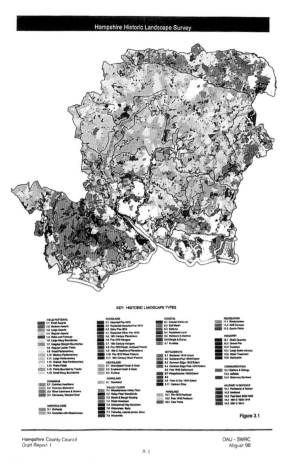

Fig 32: Hampshire: historic landscape characterisation map (by Oxford Archaeological Unit and consultants Scott Wilson)

use consultants rather than local authority staff on the main project work, and is closely linked to the Countryside Commission's *Countryside Character Map* (Countryside Commission 1998 and Agency 1999).

The planned East Anglian project, on the other hand, would bring a much closer integration of EH's national settlement map regions, and will also be the prelude to a landscape-scale MPP evaluation of field systems and their archaeology in this part of the eastern dispersed settlement province.

Overview of effectiveness

All these projects, whether completed or just beginning, have confirmed that the historic landscape characterisation methodology as pioneered in Cornwall following the *Historic Landscape Project* is a practical method within reach of available resources, technology, and levels of knowledge. It extends understanding and interpretation of the landscape, but it does not call for a greater amount of data than already exists, nor does it require extensive fieldwork or data collection. The resultant map, however, provides a context for existing data, helps us to

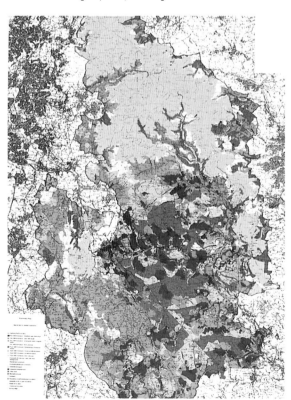

Fig 31: Peak District National Park: historic landscape characterisation map of present-day landscape (by John Barnatt for Peak District National Park)

understand the limitations of present knowledge (for example of SMR entries and their distribution see Herring and Johnson 1999), and most importantly almost automatically poses further questions about the historic landscape which can in their own right generate future research agenda and strategies.

It is also abundantly clear that the maps, whilst normally produced by archaeologists, are easily accessible to other professionals (for example planners or landscape architects) or indeed to the general public. In Cornwall it has proved its value in underpinning concepts of regional and national identity, and in integrating people's awareness of local character and origins. In the Peak National Park, it has proved to be one of the best vehicles for spreading awareness of the historic dimension and origins of the Park's well-known landscape, and in particular for linking up with habitat-based ecological mapping. In Hampshire, the project was designed from the outset to provide time-depth and historic characterisation in a form suitable to be used in direct conjunction with the county's own landscape character areas, which in turn are directly related to both the Countryside Commission's Countryside Character Areas (Countryside Commission Countryside Commission 1998 and Agency 1999) and English Nature's Natural Areas (English Nature 1997–8), and to more detailed landscape areas defined at district level.

Finally, experience in several counties has demonstrated not only the general flexibility of the historic landscape characterisation approach, particularly its capacity to achieve multiple objectives, but in addition its sensitivity to local needs, notably the ability to adapt to local circumstances, for example by employing different typologies. It thus fulfils the aims of the characterisation approach described in Chapter 9.

While embracing flexibility in this way, the technique will still in future allow different county maps to be brought together into a national map, because the techniques used share an underlying set of principles and approaches. It will be important to continue to foster this compatibility alongside more local diversity. National compatibility can also be attained by placing historic landscape character maps within other national frameworks.

At the same time as English Heritage's work has been progressing, we have given some help to the Countryside Character Programme, which has produced a national characterisation of the present landscape using a wide range of factors and variables. The national characterisation of cultural attributes, most notably probably those recording the density and pattern of fields, and

the impact on the present landscape of large-scale past industrial activity, will in particular open new areas of work. An even greater impact will be produced as the wide-ranging results of the MPP's settlement project (Roberts and Wrathmell 1995 and forthcoming) start to be applied as a framework for broader historic landscape assessments. Some of the insights it affords into regional spatial patterns and chronological trajectories of landscape development will be particularly significant. This is already happening, for example, in work on the archaeology of open field farming in the East Midlands. The Roberts/Wrathmell sub-division of England into major zones of nucleated settlement on largely cleared land and dispersed settlement in woodland regions, with its many more local sub-divisions and the strong signs that the structure or pattern revealed has very early origins, will sit very usefully above the more detailed, and more holistic, county historic landscape maps.

The work summarised in this chapter has taken about five years to achieve. At this level of detail England is a diverse, huge, place, and any ambition to extend historic landscape characterisation to the whole country (and eventually to revisit and strengthen counties already assessed) will be a daunting one, even if greater availability and increasingly sophisticated GIS can help. On the other hand the ultimate benefits of a simple, easily explained, locally-sensitive interpretation of the historic dimension of the present-day landscape of England (out of which can grow improved management of change, more focussed influence on land use, greater public awareness and support, and an ever-growing understanding of the country's archaeological resource) make this an aim worth pursuing.

It is important, nevertheless, to recognise that this review is merely a description of work in progress. Some of the ideas thrown up by the project may not immediately be taken further, but the central conclusions will remain valid as a framework for future work at national, regional, and county level. Through the current English Heritage/local authority programme they have already fuelled the development and implementation of projects such as Cornwall and its successors. The principal uncertainty lies at the very local scale, eg individual parishes, where further methodological work is needed to determine whether or not any fine-grained pattern can be recognised or whether more conventional archaeological approaches to spatial analysis and site location might remain most appropriate. Early work in Wiltshire, and in follow-up projects in Cornwall is encouraging.

Conclusion

The main principles which will most effectively guide future conservation of the historic landscape can be summarised under three heads: landscape character, sustainability, and localness.

Landscape character: the necessity of focusing on the historic dimension and character of the present-day landscape rather than only on reconstructing past landscape.

This approach carries with it the corollary of taking account of other attributes of the landscape, which may not be traditionally archaeological, such as current ecology or cultural appreciation. Within this process, however, a clear understanding of the history and archaeology of today's landscape will be essential for formulating policies and programmes to shape the future landscape.

Sustainability: an awareness of historic landscape as a critical and central component of sustainability.

Whether through the planning system, or in terms of agricultural and other land use, it is at landscape level that concepts such as environmental capital, character, and carrying capacity can most readily find meaning. It is also the scale at which ideas such as sense of place, local identity, and quality of life and environment can most effectively be defined. Archaeology is relevant to sustainable development, both in terms of helping to understand long-term environmental change and the effect of human actions, and in terms of society's need to ensure that future generations can understand their past. At both levels it is through landscape-scale work that archaeology can best interact with sustainability.

Localness: the acceptance that all landscape has some historic dimension leads to a recognition of the need to appreciate the localness of historic landscape character.

Some specific landscape areas of course are regarded as 'special' for a particular reason, but all areas have their own distinct local landscape character and diversity. It is at this local scale that land use decisions are most often taken, and at which people and communities most readily relate to the existence of the historic environment around them. Characterisation should be applied to all areas, and experience in areas such as Cornwall or Derbyshire of using historic landscape assessment to inform planning or other resource management strategies confirms that this is a practical way forward. There is no need, nor is it practical, to select particular areas for a national register. In sustainability terms, historic landscape is 'constant': selective designation and controls will function best at the level of components of the landscape which can be valued in terms of their contribution to character, but we should hesitate to be selective at landscape level.

These three headings together point the way ahead. The overall lesson to emerge from the work reported here is that the priority must be for greater understanding of the whole landscape not for the designation of selected parts of it. The county-level maps described in this chapter, and the approach defined by the wider *Historic Landscape Project*, give a robust and practical method of achieving this understanding. The aim should be to provide the means to promote awareness of all the many ways in which the landscape has been changed over long time-periods The desirable longer-term aim is not to attempt to halt change but promote a greater awareness among land users and managers of the need to ensure that there is a considered and beneficial process the use of which will help us to plan which particular type of landscape we hand on to future generations – that is to shape tomorrow's landscape.

Historic landscape characterisation or assessment can identify what is characteristic, fundamental, or important in an area and explain why it is there, thus helping informed and sympathetic discussion about what should be changed and what conserved. It will thereby be an important tool for guiding future change to build on what now exists and to retain historic diversity in the environment.

Landowners, local communities, government, and local authorities will all obviously wish to identify what is different, special, and above all characteristic, in their own areas and regions, and the method of historic landscape characterisation described above has been developed to help them to do this. It does not prescribe what is important, nor try to define value from only one perspective. In most cases, however, the things which most contribute to local character or to sense of place will be found to be of historic origin, that is, to be the result of the human actions and activities which have taken place there in the past. The results of recent work, whose fuller publication will follow, have demonstrated that an effective, practical, and affordable method of large-scale historic landscape characterisation now exists. The various approaches and methods summarised above will help to establish the historic character of an area. These need now to be applied more widely throughout the country. They are not intended to be used in order to take a purely protectionist stance, but rather to develop awareness of the values inherited from the past so as to utilise what is best and most characteristic about them to create tomorrow's landscape.

Annex 1: A methodological test in Kent: sampling and quantification

Paul Chadwick

Introduction

The Kent project was designed in the context of *This common inheritance* and English Heritage's 1991 *Consultation Paper* (*see chapter 1*) to test a specific approach to historic landscape identification and assessment in advance of the main *Historic Landscape Project*, and to explore a number of loosely interconnected themes which, if appropriate, could be taken forward by future projects. The project methodology was evolved during October and November 1992 and was implemented between December 1992 and July 1993.

Definition of the Kent test project

One approach to historic landscape identification under active consideration in 1992 was to place such assessments within a framework set by a regional scale zoning of the landscape. Such an approach, if successful, would then enable future historic landscape assessments to dovetail into the framework emerging from the Countryside Commission's *New Map* (Countryside Commission 1994), which at that at date was a pilot study undertaken during 1992–3 in south west England (*see chapter 2 above*). In contrast, the Kent project sought to complement a regional zoning of the landscape with a detailed methodological study within and across regional and sub-regional landscape boundaries. The Kent project envisaged a macro level zoning of the landscape, within which historic landscape studies could then characterise and identify the historic element at a micro level.

The study aimed to :

- cover all historic elements of the countryside within the sample area (not merely individual components or features of archaeological or historic interest)

- consider, briefly, definitions and professional perceptions of historic landscape

- explore opportunities presented by computer manipulation of historic landscape related data

- classify various archaeological and ecological elements of the landscape into categories

- explore the relevance of using the Secretary of State's non-statutory criteria (developed for the assessment of ancient monuments) and attempt to identify relevant weightings and scorings of the various categories

- test the grading of landscape into a four part classification: national, regional, local, and residual

- examine relationships between historic landscape and existing statutory designations

Kent was selected for the study for a variety of reasons. It enjoys a diverse range of geological and topographic zones each supporting visually, ecologically, and archaeologically varied landscapes. More importantly these zones are already widely recognised and documented by Kent County Council, (see for instance Kent County Council 1983 and Kent County Council 1993) and might reasonably be expected to form the basis for the Countryside Commission's Countryside character maps or similar zoning of this region. Additionally, Kent County Council have systematically and comprehensively surveyed, documented and classified the County's ecology through a GIS. The county SMR was machine based, it included scheduled monuments but did not incorporate a systematic survey of the resource. Historic building data was in hard copy format: *DoE List of Buildings of Special Architectural or Historic Interest* or (Green Backs) and a card index for other historic buildings and farms. There was also perceived to be a wealth of historic landscape-related data available for the county.

Sample areas

The aims of this project required the careful selection of areas to be sampled, and to this end the assistance of Dr Linda Davis (Kent County Council Ecologist) and Dr John Williams (Kent County Council Archaeologist) is gratefully acknowledged. Six areas were identified, each 25 sq km in extent (ie each area comprised a

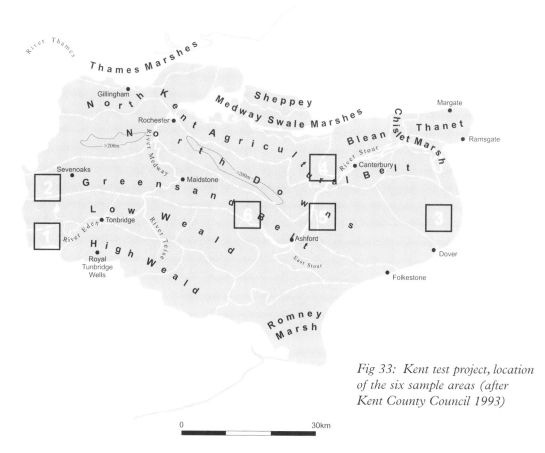

Fig 33: Kent test project, location of the six sample areas (after Kent County Council 1993)

0   30km

1:10,000 Ordnance Survey Sheet) making an overall total of 150 sq km. The areas were located in a non-random manner across the county, within and, in most instances, across the boundaries of the Landscape Character Areas (LCA) defined by Kent County Council, 1993 (Fig 33). The sample areas, positioned specifically to avoid the various coastal zones, were targeted to study samples of the High Weald, the Low Weald, the Greensand Belt, Chalk Downland, the 'Blean' area of north Kent, and the so called Kent Agricultural Belt.

The only constraint imposed on data selection was the exclusion of all features less than fifty years old. Such features (ie post *c*1943) were not classified or scored. Essentially, then, all traces of man's activities on the landscape up to 1943 were included and assessed (cf Morgan-Evans 1985).

Within these six areas preconceived definitions of what comprised historic landscape were deliberately avoided. Instead, by exploring and scoring the data in various ways the project sought to detect and identify relevant historic elements of the landscape. The approach was thus to work upwards and outwards from basic landscape components, (elsewhere called bottom-up) rather than from already available definitions (top-down) (*see chapter 4, Initial review, stage 2, and chapters 7 and 8*). Each sample area was selected for a particular set of attributes.

Sample area 1, in the High Weald LCA: The Wadhurst Clays produce a rolling topography with steep sided wooded valleys. Between wooded valleys there is a pattern of small irregular shaped fields. Settlement is essentially nucleated in villages which present a sixteenth-century appearance, but otherwise settlement is confined to isolated farm dwellings or hamlets of two or three cottages. 98% of the area lies within an AONB and listed buildings, SSSIs, Sites of Nature Conservation Interest (SNCIs) and Ancient Woodlands are common. The area also includes a small part of the Low Weald. Key features to be examined were the contribution of Ancient Woodland to the historic landscape, the pattern and density of field boundaries and shaws, and the evidence for the former iron industry.

Sample area 2, in the Low Weald and Greensand Belt LCAs: contained elements of the Lower Greensand scarp and the Vale of Holmesdale. Geologically varied, with Holmesdale comprising Gault Clays, Lower Greensand and Hythe Beds providing hilly topography, and Atherfield Clays and Weald Clays towards the southern part of the area supporting a more undulating relief. Land use is similarly varied, with rich mixed farming in Holmesdale, dense beech woodland on the Greensand with occasional heath and small irregular fields, and the Low Weald characterised by less wooded, enclosed pasture fields. Settlement is infrequent and dispersed: 90% of the area is within an AONB and Ancient Woodland, SNCIs, and listed buildings are present. Features to be tested by scoring included the contribution of hedgerows, copses, and woodlands, former green lanes, a modest range of SMR evidence, and the contribution of historic parks and gardens to the historic landscape.

Sample area 3, in the North Downs LCA: situated in the intensively farmed (arable) chalk Downland. Only 3% of the area is within an AONB. Ancient Woodland is rare and other conservation designations are virtually non-existent. In contrast, the SMR contains a wealth of evidence of prehistoric and Roman settlement, field systems, and burial activity, although all are sub-surface features. The line of the Roman road from Dover to Canterbury crosses the area still utilised in parts as footpaths, green lanes, and minor roads. Settlement is sparse but is concentrated in three small historic nucleated settlements. Here the project sought to examine the possible conflicts between time depth and lack of visibility presented by the (largely) buried archaeological/historic landscape.

Sample area 4, in The Blean and North Kent Agricultural Belt LCAs: The Blean comprises London Clay and heavy acidic soils which support dense chestnut and oak woodland. In contrast the agricultural belt comprises fine fertile sands and loams which support a landscape of orchards, small woods, and arable fields. The project sought to examine the effects of a specific type of modern agricultural regime (fruit growing) on the historic landscape and to examine the ecologically rich Blean and the apparently limited impact of man on this landscape.

Sample area 5, in the Greensand Belt and North Downs LCAs: topographically varied ranging from the level flood plain of the Great Stow to the steep slopes of the Chalk Downland. Land use is similarly varied with mixed farming on the Greensand deposits in marked contrast to the woodland, grassland, and arable mix of the Downs. Within this sample area was the historic town of Wye, otherwise settlement generally comprised single farmsteads. Virtually all the area (99.8%) is within an AONB. Chalk grasslands formed extensive SSSIs and several archaeological sites are scheduled monuments. Here the project sought to examine the implications of larger settlements on historic landscape assessment and the historic landscape 'value' of large areas of ancient grassland.

Sample area 6, in the Weald and Greensand Belt LCAs: the Low Weald is level or gently undulating with a mixture of pasture and arable farming. A pronounced scarp, in places a cliff, marks the transition to the Lower Greensand Hythe Beds. Hedgerow removal has occurred and orchards are extensive, to the north of the area the topography becomes more undulating, with sand deposits supporting remnants of heath and coniferous plantation. The area is also impacted by the M20, the Folkestone to London railway and mineral workings. Only 1% of the area is within an AONB, but the eastern sector of the area is classified as a Special Landscape Area. Ancient Woodland is present in localised areas and SNCIs/SSSIs protect several waterside habitats along the Great Stow.

Methods

Seven data sources were trawled in order to assess all historic elements of the landscape within each sample area, and all relevant data scored. These were:

- Kent Wildlife Habitat Survey. A database (GIS compatible) containing biological survey data collected to the English Nature Phase 1 survey methodology (Nature Conservancy Council 1990)

- Kent Sites and Monuments Record (SMR)

- DoE List of Buildings of Special Architectural or Historic Interest 'Green Backs'

- Kent Farmstead Survey. An architectural description, photographic record, and chronological analysis of a sample of farmsteads threatened by neglect or redevelopment (Kent County Council nd)

- Historic Parks and Gardens. Kent County Council have undertaken and published a comprehensive survey of historic parks and gardens (Kent County Council 1992a and 1992b) providing descriptive, spatial, and chronological data

- Place name evidence. Although not studied by the English Place-Name Society, a number of researchers have worked on the cartographic, documentary and linguistic origins of Kent place-names (Wallenberg 1931, 1934 and Everitt 1986)

- Development Plans. Relevant Structure, Local and Subject Plans were examined to establish the nature and extent of landscape related policies (for example Kent County Council 1983)

In order to provide a framework for a rigorous and consistent scoring system a classification system which encompassed all elements of the historic landscape was required. An early attempt to provide a categorisation had been provided by Morgan Evans (1985). This proposed a three-fold classification: archaeology, hedgerows, and woods. Whilst this approach had the benefit of crossing existing artificial boundaries between databases and specialist disciplines, the failure to include the built element of the historic landscape suggested that further refinement and development of this categorisation was required. A more recent examination of the classification of features of archaeological, nature conservation and landscape interest was presented by Lambrick (1992a). This approach, based on 'state of preservation rather than any automatic chronological distinction', took an ambiguous stance to certain elements of the landscape. For instance, Lambrick flags concerns that 'the sheer number of field boundaries could heavily weight the overall assessment'. It was to address this very problem of balance and weighting that English Heritage's 1991 Consultation Paper presented a new classificatory approach.

This revised classification proposed that various elements of the landscape (regardless of data source) be sorted into several categories: sub-surface features, earthworks, unroofed structures and ruins, roofed structures, field boundaries, historic, and natural features (redefined and re-titled semi-natural habitats during the course of the Kent project). This categorisation is clearly based on the form and state of preservation of features within the landscape rather than an attempt to reflect their antiquity. However any perceived chronological shortcomings were balanced by the specific scoring of the chronological element of each feature within the landscape.

One element of the Kent pilot tested an alternative classification and scoring based on function (agricultural, transportation, industrial, natural). This approach had the positive benefit of grouping related features; for example farmhouse, farm buildings, field boundaries; and could, if applied on a larger scale, accommodate long distance settlement and economic dynamics for example farmhouse/market town relationships, but it was felt on review by the steering group that the approach was over simplistic and was not tested beyond one sample area.

The English Heritage's 1991 classification was therefore adopted by the Kent project. One of the

principal aims was to trial the relevance of its categories and to test them against the Secretary of State's non-statutory criteria by the application of a scoring system. Mindful of the pitfalls of overly complex scoring systems and future options for machine based manipulation and scoring of data, wherever possible a yes/no (score/no score) system was developed.

For each element of the Secretary of State's criteria (period, rarity, documentation, survival, diversity, fragility potential and group value) a scoring system was developed. For instance, period information was accorded an ascending score with twentieth-century features scoring 0.5, eighth-century features scoring 7.5, and Neolithic features 25. As might be anticipated, archaeological evidence for sub-surface and earthwork features scored well on chronological grounds, whereas ecological features (considered within the semi-natural-habitats class) generally scored 0.5 (twentieth century unless greater antiquity could be demonstrated). Thus ancient woodland scored a higher mark, typically 2 or more, and the rare instances of boundaries documented in Anglo-Saxon charters scored 7.5 if an eighth-century date was suggested.

Although this is not the place to detail fully the scoring system, this chapter presents a commentary on the results which enables the workings of the scoring to be demonstrated. Scoring, weighting and analysis was undertaken on a 1km grid drawn from the national grid. Each sample area comprised a 5 x 5km grid and this was used as the basis for the analysis of patterns of scores within each category of data within and between each sample area, patterns from permutations of scores within each sample area, and patterns of total scores within and between sample area.

Analysis of results

It was evident, even from the most rudimentary analysis of scores, that results reflected to a reasonable degree the historic landscape character of each sample area. Sample area 1 selected for its extensive ancient woodland, pattern of historic fields (most defined by an ecologically rich hedgerows) and historic villages scored particularly well in the relevant categories (semi-natural habitats and roofed structures). Archaeologically the area is not renowned for its prehistoric or Roman evidence and relevant categories (sub-surface features and earthworks) scored poorly (Table 8). In contrast sample area 3, selected for its wealth of sub-surface features (evidenced by cropmarks), scored well in that category, but low in other aspects such as ecology and historic buildings (Table 9).

Table 8: Kent historic landscape assessment, test project. Sample area 1, Low and High Weald

Sub-surface features

	2.5			
2.5				15
11.5		5		
2.5	5.5			

Earthworks

				1
	5		2.5	2.5

Roofed structures
Cowden Village

45	41	48.5	9.5	14
12	13		9	35.5
	6.5	28	18	25
8	27.5	9.5	9	24
14.5	100.59	10.5	2	

Field boundaries

26.5	33	36.5	19	14
13	15	11.5	13.5	14
14.5	16.5	25	16	19.5
11	16	18	16.5	26
21	37	17.5	5.5	14

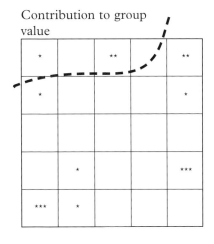

Historical and natural features

19	48	54	30.5	62
72.5	47	48	40.5	53.5
60	49	41	35.5	81
55.5	36	33.5	56.5	62.5
70	56.5	22.5	9.5	19.5

Contribution to group value

*		**		**
*				*
	*			***
***	*			

Total score

90.5	122	139	59	90
97.5	77.5	59.5	63	103
77	72	94	69.5	141.5
86	79.5	66	82	112.5
108	213.5	50.5	19.5	39

Table 9: Kent historic landscape assessment test project. Sample area 3

Sub-surface features

95	115	221	208	167.5
96	249	220	51	79
72	114	111.5	51	104
51	163	150	143.5	22
29	74	47	58	326

Earthworks

				9
		6		

Roofed structures
Cowden Village

			45.5	11.5
			11	9.5
	19.5		9.5	
	4	20.5	39.5	1
	12.5		18	

Field boundaries

2.5	14.5	8	14	9
13.5	22	11	14	7.5
0.5	26.5	20	14	7
9	7	15.5	14	11.5
7.5	22.5	6.5	14	6.5

Historical and
natural features

12.5	13.5	4.5	26	
19	12	6.5	3.5	7.5
8	23	21	13.5	5
	15	55	16	12.5
1	25	7.5	7	5

Contribution to
group value

		*	*	
			*	
*		*		
		*	*	
	*		*	

Total score

110	143	233.5	293.5	188
128.5	283	237.5	79.5	122.5
80.5	183	152.5	88	116
60	189	198.5	213	47
37.5	134	61	97	337.5

It was clear, at a glance, that the scores reflected real differences between the historic character of each sample area and that in many cases key characteristics within an area could be identified by high (or low) scores

The project then moved on to examine whether scoring was subtle enough (andimplicitly the categorisation and scoring system sound enough) to detect boundaries between landscape character zones already identified by established assessment techniques

(cf Kent County Council 1993). Despite the random nature of the superimposition of the National Grid onto the landscape, and the fact that there was no obvious or natural boundary line delimiting each character zone, the examination of individual category scores and aggregated totals produced positive results. Table 10 presents total scores for all the sample areas. The relationship of the sample areas to the *County Council's Landscape Character Areas* is shown in Fig 33.

Table 10: Kent historic landscape project. Sample areas 1–6, total scores with landscape character areas (Kent County Council 1993) superimposed

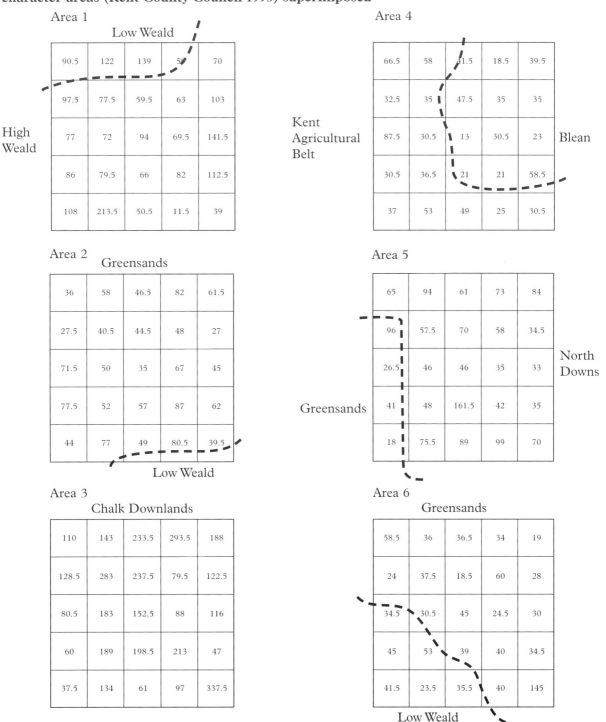

The following section selects only three of the six sample areas and highlights and interprets scores which assist in defining the character of each zone and point to boundaries between zones.

Sample area 1: The divide between the Low and High Weald character areas was barely evident on the basis of the total scores. However, when the scores for individual classes were examined the divide became more apparent. Field boundary and roofed structures were scored higher in Low Weald than in adjacent High Weald areas, while historic and natural features (retitled semi-natural habitats) scores were more variable but tended to be below the sample area average in the Low Weald.

Sample area 2: the divide between Holmesdale and the Greensands was identified on the basis of lower total scores in Holmesdale. Similarly, the divide between Greensands and Low Weald although sinuous and difficult to define on the ground could tentatively be identified by low scores at the bottom right and left corners of the grid. Again, field boundary scores suggest zone boundaries should be sought towards the top left and bottom right corners, an impression strengthened by scores for roofed structures and semi-natural habitats.

Sample area 6: a boundary is identifiable (whilst not detectable on total scores) on the basis of higher scores for Structures and Ruins, higher Field Boundary scores, which characterise the Greensand Belt, while lower scores for historic and natural features define the Low Weald from its adjacent zone.

Notable is the regular occurrence of high scores in area 3. These highlight a particular problem, that of extensive and ancient sub-surface (cropmark) features which score well on chronological grounds. Clearly this evidence is relevant in demonstrating that an extensive open landscape has been in place for several millennia (the open character of this historic landscape is thus a key characteristic), however given the lack of visible evidence (from ground level at least) and the paucity of other valuable ecological or built features it was considered necessary to negatively weight sub-surface features. A number of the steering group members suggested that all non-visible (archaeological) features should be excluded from the scoring, others felt this would ignore an important element providing time-depth evidence within the landscape. Negative weighting appeared an acceptable compromise.

One of the initial aims of this project was to grade the various sample areas and to classify them in terms of relative importance. The project presented a number of gradings for raw score totals (for example including cropmark related scores), totals for individual classes (for example field boundaries), and weighted total scores. A significant hierarchy of scores emerged with landscape already recognised for their scenic, historic, and ecological interest emerging well clear of other less rich or diverse landscape.

Conclusions

From a diverse agenda to explore a number of loosely interconnected themes, the Kent test project established some important benchmarks for future historic landscape projects. It established the relevance of considering all traces of human activities on the landscape, it demonstrated the usefulness of several existing data bases as a tool to identifying key characteristics of the historic landscape and it proved that in terms of indirect assessment, a 'number crunching' approach to historic landscape identification was feasible (although it would have considerable resource implications unless machine manipulation of data bases by GIS is more widely available).

This experiment highlighted widespread preconceptions and misconceptions amongst planning officers and other professionals, suggesting that the concept of historic landscape had still to be more clearly defined. More positively, it proved that the Secretary of State's criteria for the assessment of ancient monuments, if it is applied alongside professional judgement, are robust enough for use in the assessment of historic landscape. Overall this very detailed approach to historic landscape identification was shown to be a valid approach and (subject to further refinement) capable of application elsewhere. It would however, probably be most useful for comparing distinct areas by means of proxy indicators, and normally within a framework provided by more comprehensive landscape characterisation.

Acknowlegements

Paul Chadwick is grateful to the members of the project Steering Group: Graham Fairclough (English Heritage), John Williams and Linda Davies (Kent County Council), and Keith Selmes (English Nature); for helpful discussion, but more generally to all those officers of Kent County Council Planning Department and the staff of the Museum of Kentish Life who gave a great deal of assistance to the project.

Annex 2: Historic landscape characterisation in Cornwall

Peter Herring

Introduction

What is the best way to conserve the complex mix of cultural and semi-natural features which constitute the historic landscape (ie those elements of the landscape created by people), and the multitude of personal and communal historic meanings which give it its value? Is it a simple choice between statutory constraint by the designation of 'important' parts of the historic landscape, or a more organic and *bottom-up* form of conservation which develops from positive management strategies and from encouraging people to understand, appreciate, respect and celebrate those parts of the historic landscape they live, work and play in? Can there be a fruitful mixing of the two approaches?

Some historic buildings and archaeological areas or sites already receive a degree of protection through statutory designations such as listed buildings, scheduled monuments, conservation areas or *Areas of Great Historic Value* (Cornwall's Structure Plan designation), and others will receive it through English Heritage's MPP and its *Register of Historic Parks and Gardens* and *Register of Historic Battlefields*. Most of the historic landscape of Cornwall (and the rest of England), however is, or will be, missed by this selective high-constraint approach, since even statutorily designated buildings, sites, and areas often receive limited protection, based on how general or particular are the emphases of the recorded descriptions of them, and on the criteria used to evaluate their importance. Their character and historic meaning may be eroded by actions with break no laws or planning rules. Closely drawn constraints can also fail to protect the context of a feature, and the value of the feature itself can be impoverished if damaging changes are made to the land around it. While much can be protected through planning policies and processes in association with designation, most of the rural landscape and potential changes to that landscape are outside the scope of the planning process.

It may be argued that the key to landscape (as opposed to site) conservation and management lies not in designation and protection but in encouraging wide recognition that the historic landscape and its components have value not only to historians and archaeologists, but also to the whole community. The complex and deep-rooted relationships that individuals and communities develop with the cultural and semi-natural worlds which they inhabit, and through which they identify and give value to themselves, mean that they often have much more to lose and thus more reason to conserve the character of their environment than do historians and archaeologists.

Perhaps we need to continually emphasise that the historic landscape includes not just particular identified features, but also the general fabric of the environment, and not just those features deliberately created but also those formed incidentally to peoples' actions or by historic processes, often in unexpected ways. So the historic landscape contains not only the home and its yard, but also the field boundaries and the land contained by them, the lonely wayside cross and the windswept common it stands on. It will also include the rutted hollow-ways and the acid heath, growing on the soils which were commons impoverished by over-use 3000 years ago, the woods colonising a great nineteenth-century quarry, and the plant and animal communities which have developed in estuaries silted with medieval tinners' waste.

There is clearly a need to continue raising the profile of the historic landscape in all debates concerning the future of the landscape, for instance ensuring that it is fully considered in general landscape assessments, in discussions about potentially damaging proposals, or when countryside managers plan what they intend to be benign changes. The Cornwall Archaeological Unit (CAU), like other archaeological 'curators' in local authorities elsewhere in England, would like to be able to attend and where appropriate give advice to each evening meeting of the 200 or so Cornish parish councils when they discuss issues like the siting of a mobile phone aerial on the last heathy downland in the parish, the diversion of an ancient path, or the insertion of dormer windows into houses where they have not previously been part of the vocabulary of the region's vernacular architecture. It would like to be involved in discussions between land agents and tenants about re-introducing sheep to Zennor cliffs, or to be in a position to dissuade a farmer from spending an afternoon removing a 600-years-old Cornish hedge, or the last fragment of a wood which had been carefully managed for 4000 years. Informed archaeological opinion should be present at every decisive encounter or critical moment, but local authorities do not have sufficient resources to be represented either in person (or even in site-specific policy guidance) at every county or district council discussion on wide-ranging issues, such as mineral extraction, derelict land reclamation, and road and house building schemes.

If it is not possible to be directly involved at every critical moment, it is at least possible to try to be indirectly involved by providing those making the decisions with usable material to guide them. Mapping the historic landscape and providing an understandable and factual textual commentary is probably the most consistent and powerful way of providing a coherent and consistent body of advice with limited resources, in other words of providing appropriate levels of support *in absentia*.

Historic landscape characterisation

Much previous historic landscape assessment and mapping has been *top-down*; ie experienced landscape historians carefully designate specially important areas and then make efforts to establish controls limiting damaging development and promoting positive management within these area, (see Kelly 1994 for a recent exercise in which Landscapes of Special Historic Interest were identified in Wales and placed on an interim register alongside Parks and Gardens of Special Historic interest). Cornwall Archaeological Unit have been involved in such approaches in the last 15–20 years in Cornwall guiding the resources of bodies such as English Heritage, and the (former) RCHME, the Countryside Commission, the National Trust, and district councils towards recording, interpreting, and conserving extensive archaeological remains and historic landscape in particular parts of Cornwall. In order to identify those areas generally regarded as being of special historic or archaeological value:for example large areas like Bodmin Moor, West Penwith, and the Isles of Scilly, and smaller ones like the Luxulyan Valley, St Keverne, Lanhydrock estate, St Michael's Mount and Kit Hill (Johnson and Rose 1994; Ratcliffe 1989; Smith 1988; Johns and Herring 1996; Thomas 1994; Herring 1992; Herring and Thomas 1990). Parts of the historic landscape under immediate threat have also been studied specifically to help guide change; for example the St Austell China-Clay Area, and road and pipeline corridors (Herring and Smith 1991; Thomas and Rose 1990; Thomas 1992; Thomas and Johns 1995; Thomas 1996; Cole 1996).

Such an approach, an informal sort of designation, leaves an awful lot of Cornwall untouched, and would-be guardians of the historic landscape feeling troubled about the neglect of a greater part of the county which flows from concentrating effort in so-called special areas. This

is particularly troubling if we acknowledge that the whole landscape is historic, and that the whole of it needs to be managed appropriately.

The Cornwall Archaeological Unit was pleased, therefore, to be invited in 1994 to provide an assessment of the historic landscape character of the whole of Cornwall, co-funded by English Heritage. This assessment was primarily designed to inform an important Countryside Commission-sponsored landscape assessment, but it was welcomed as well by CAU and English Heritage for offering the opportunity to develop a practical and robust method of preparing the mapping and documentation of the historic landscape which would be a valuable resource for other people and organisations in the many ways indicated or inferred above.

The Cornwall Archaeological Unit worked closely and productively with Alison Farmer, Andrew Slater, and Robert Tregay of Landscape Design Associates on the project which was commissioned by the Countryside Commission with support from English Heritage, Cornwall County Council, and the six district councils. Valuable guidance was given by Graham Fairclough of English Heritage.

As the work was intended to assist in assessing present landscape character, we recorded the predominant historic character detectable in today's landscape. For different purposes we could have used other methods or different sources and mapping criteria: for instance, using the available evidence to reconstruct an aspect of historic Cornwall at one or more of its important historic moments, for example in 1840 for which parish tithe maps are a major source, or at *c*1500 to capture the late medieval landscape; or using archaeological or palaeo-environmental evidence to attempt to reconstruct earlier semi-natural or cultural landscapes. But the mapping of current historic character appears to be the most productive approach. Many other forms of historic mapping can be generated from it because the different historic landscape character types mapped are clearly the products of the landscape's complex evolution over the centuries, or of the historic processes to which it has been subjected. Historic character mapping is also useful to those individuals and bodies who are dealing with the present landscape because it provides understanding of the historic dimension and significance of the landscape we have today, rather than attempting merely to describe the landscape we used to have, or think we had. Such knowledge of the present landscape is the first step towards being able to make informed decisions about its future.

The method developed in Cornwall is described in detail elsewhere (Landscape Design

Associates and Cornwall Archaeological Unit 1994; Herring 1998, Herring and Johnson 1999), but needs to be summarised here. It extended and developed methods which CAU first used with Land Use Consultants for a pilot study undertaken earlier in 1994 of the Bodmin Moor part of the Cornwall AONB (Countryside Commission 1994c). The basic approach was to use readily-available and systematic sources to objectivise the historic landscape so that a full range of historic landscape character types could be identified, mapped, described, analysed, and where necessary subdivided or combined to create zones or, more usefully, super-types. Each parcel of land in Cornwall, down to individual fields, was assessed and ascribed to one of seventeen *Historic Landscape Character Types*, using the Ordnance Survey 1:25,000 maps reduced to 1:50,000. The range of types (see Figs 34 and 35 below) was determined before mapping began and was based on close interrogation of maps of Cornwall, coupled with the CAU's knowledge of the county. The typology was to some extent defined by the availability of countywide and consistent sources, such as the 1:10,000 habitat maps prepared by the Cornwall Wildlife Trust, the Institute of Cornish Studies' place-names maps and index, or early editions of Ordnance Survey maps showing field patterns. Access to and confidence in systematic sources is important for the success of the method. The identification of landscape types was also limited by the scale of mapping, by the resources (time) available, by the requirements of both the landscape assessment and other likely users, and finally by the need to prevent the product becoming over-complex or too detailed, in particular by avoiding 'point' or site detail.

The following broad *Historic Landscape Character Types* were defined and mapped for Cornwall:

Rough ground
Prehistoric enclosures
Medieval enclosures
Post-medieval enclosures (seventeenth to eighteenth century)
Modern enclosures
Ancient woodland
Plantations and scrub
Settlements (pre-twentieth century)
Settlements (twentieth century)
Industrial (active)
Industrial (relict)
Communications (roads, airfields etc)
Recreation
Military
Ornamental
Reservoirs
Natural water-bodies

It took 60 person-days to assemble and interpret the sources to map these types for the whole of Cornwall at a rate of 60 sq km per day, creating a very detailed mosaic of types. This mosaic was, as noted above, interpreted and to some extent simplified into even broader patterns through a process of generalising including combining some types (for example the post-medieval and modern enclosure types became the super-type/zone recently enclosed land). Other types were subdivided to make them more understandable (rough ground for instance became dunes, coastal rough ground and upland rough ground) and a number of zones were recognised where it was felt that topography overrode type in determining historic character: for eaxample steep-sided valleys, navigable rivers and creeks, and the inter-tidal zone. The mapping of supertypes or zones was thus still relatively objective, with most being directly derived from the Historic Landscape Character Types but with some intervening interpretation. This higher-level was felt to be the most useful level of mapping for understanding, presenting. and managing the historic landscape.

The eighteen simplified types or zones identified for Cornwall were:

Upland rough ground
Coastal rough ground
Dunes
Anciently enclosed land (AEL)
AEL significantly altered in the eighteenth and nineteenth centuries
AEL significantly altered in the twentieth century
Recently enclosed land
Navigable rivers and creeks
teep-sided valleys
Urban development
Ornamental
Recreation
Industrial
Military
Airfields
Upland woods (plantations)
Reservoirs
Inter-tidal

Detailed supporting text was prepared for each of these simplified types. These texts were designed to deal with potential users' needs for description, interpretation, evaluation and suggested management, and followed a set format of the twenty sections listed:

• Introduction, including basic defining/ distinguishing attributes.

- Principal historic processes that have produced or affected the zone. Includes an identification of key periods.

- Typical historic/archaeological components and features found within the zone.

- Rarity, in regional and national terms, of the zone and of the typical historic components, or complexes of components.

- Statement on typical survival of historic or archaeological components within the zone.

- Statement concerning degree of surviving coherence of the historic components, from various periods.

- Nature and extent of past interaction of land use and other uses/functions of this zone with other zones.

- Visibility and coherence of evidence for time-depth.

- Contribution of historic landscape character to the present landscape character.

- Values and perceptions of the zone.

- Quality and extent of archaeological and historic research and documentation for the zone.

- The potential offered by the zone for historic or archaeological research.

- The potential the zone offers those concerned with amenity and education.

- Statement concerning typical condition of historic or archaeological components within the zone.

- Vulnerability of components. To include a brief review of typical statutory designations or other forms of protection.

- Forces for change within the zone. To include forces for conservation as well as destruction or damage.

- Summary statement of the zone's importance.

- Principal locations of the zone in Cornwall.

- Extent and nature of variability within the zone through Cornwall.

- A brief statement on recommended landscape management for the zone.

Time-depth and component or feature matrices were prepared for each zone. These matrices were based on those devised by Cobham Resource Consultants and Oxford Archaeological Unit (1993, and Table 7 above) but they were elaborated with advice from Landscape Design Associates to attempt to show how much impact landscape features from particular periods may have had on landscape character.

We were also asked to evaluate or grade zones, a rather invidious process as it tends to prevent all zones being managed appropriately without privileging some over others. This uneasiness was partly alleviated by grading the zones for a number of criteria and stressing that each was of similar importance so that zones with low overall gradings might still score well in certain areas.

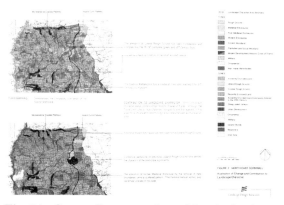

Fig 34: Cornwall: extract from historic landscape characterisation map showing types and simplified types, and simple characterisation (from LDA and CAU 1994)

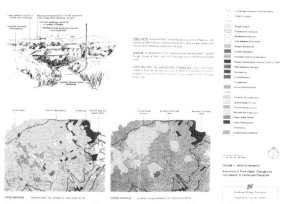

Fig 35: Cornwall: extract from historic landscape characterisation map showing types and simplified types, and simple characterisation using sketches (from LDA and CAU 1994)

A final, rather separate, stage of the assessment involved mapping *Historic Landscape Character Areas*, mainly to help guide Landscape Design Associates's selection of Landscape Character Areas. A total of fifty *Historic Landscape Character Areas* (Figs 34 and 35) were named and given summary descriptions which included the justification for separating them out as discrete parts of Cornwall's historic landscape. There are however problems with accepting the boundaries and internal integrity of areas. This is especially the case when, as in Cornwall, several criteria, not all generated by the characterisation process outlined above, were used to determine areas. Some were defined by the remains of relatively short-term historic episodes (for example the Redruth–Camborne tin and copper mining area) while neighbouring areas (for example the uplands of Carnmenellis) were drawn from the character types and mainly represented long term agricultural land-use patterns. Critical examination of the areas might produce overlapping or fuzzy-edged areas, difficult for planners and landscape managers to work with, but more closely reflecting reality.

Defining the *Historic Landscape Character Areas* was as close as the Cornish assessment came to designation. Care was taken, however, not to add valuations of relative importance to the brief commentaries prepared for these areas, to ensure that the assessment could not be used as a designation exercise. It was felt that the characterisation of the landscape into types and super-types/zones was more objective, more flexible or capable of adjustment, more rooted in reality, and more readily owned by the user, than designation which is more subjective; more vague or fuzzy but yet more fixed, created by and thus belonging to someone else. The attempt to define *Historic Landscape Character Areas* was not carried further, and it was the map of types, used to inform the county landscape assessment, which lay at the heart of the overall project.

Application of the Cornwall *Historic Landscape Character Assessment*

Alison Farmer and Andrew Slater of Landscape Design Associates made full and good use of the mapping, text, and matrices at all stages of their landscape assessment work: in their pre-fieldwork desk study; in their fieldwork; in the identification of their landscape character areas; and in the four detailed and influential reports they prepared (Landscape Design Associates 1994; Landscape Design Associates and Cornwall Archaeological Unit 1994; Cornwall County Council 1996; Countryside Commission, forthcoming).

There was immediate feedback at the fieldwork stage of Landscape Design Associate's work when it was apparent that two extensive zones, anciently and recently enclosed land, were not as easily distinguishable as had been expected, at least as originally described to Landscape Design Associates. The main problem was that a key feature defining of most recently enclosed land, its ruler straight boundaries, as recorded on maps or graphic records, is less perceptible on the ground because of the distortions created by Cornwall's undulating topography. Although superficially similar, the two zones have fundamentally different histories and characteristics, as well as different management needs and threats to their character. It was therefore important to modify the information provided for Landscape Design Associates so that visual differences could be defined more effectively. Greater attention was drawn to differences in scale and form of field boundaries, typical vegetation, communities growing on and alongside them, and the positioning and form of settlements, while the most typical indicators of relative poverty, past and present, in the more marginal recently enclosed land, and relative wealth in the anciently enclosed land, were defined.

The text and matrices helped Landscape Design Associates to describe time-depth and landscape change within their *Landscape Character Areas*, allowed them to present summaries of the development of historic character within these areas and draw attention to typical features. It enabled them to see more clearly the forces for change inherent in the landscape through more fully understanding the historic trajectories which create it, and also to appreciate the impact on historic character that externally imposed changes would have. This led to Landscape Design Associates being able to more fully incorporate historic concerns into their detailed recommendations, some of which will inform or become future district or county council planning policies, and National Trust or Cornwall Heritage Trust acquisition policies. Others will guide the targeting of positive management such as MAFF's Countryside Stewardship scheme or countryside access agreements.

The Cornwall landscape assessment has now been published, with a large, well-produced version of the historic landscape character zones map (Cornwall County Council 1996). It has been distributed to all local government planning officers, forward planners and development control officers in all six district councils in Cornwall as well as to county council staff including particularly Countryside officers and the County Surveyor. In addition copies have been given to other users, including MAFF, English Nature, Countryside Commission, Environment Agency, National Trust, Country Landowners Association, Forestry Commission, and Campaign or the Preservation of Rural England. Copies for public use have also been deposited in county libraries, and further work has been commissioned by English Heritage to publish the map and its supporting text in an attractive, accessible, format in order to ensure that the map reaches a much wider audience (Herring 1998).

Cornwall Archaeological Unit staff can now, by means of the report and the map, provide a coherent and consistent body of information and advice to influence decision-making for proposals and actions which will have impact on the historic landscape and its future, even if resources prevent us from being directly involved in every discussion and meeting   in other words, we can be 'present while absent'. It is still too early to comment on how councillors, officers, and countryside managers have used the information, but the detailed types and zones mapping, and a final draft of the report, have been part of the Cornwall Archaeological Unit archive for over two years. The development control officers on the curatorial side of the Unit use the report and map regularly to prepare advice for the County Archaeologist concerning the likely impact of proposed developments on the components or the character of the historic landscape. The principal message of the map is that all areas are in some way historic, that it is possible to identify the main components of any type of landscape, and that it is possible, therefore, to take steps to encourage the preservation of these essential components where there is a desire to conserve the character of an area. The breakthrough has been to clearly identify for the first time what these components are. Once these are known it is possible to take meaningful decisions as to their future.

The anciently-enclosed-land zone covers c60% of the whole county and is one of the main subjects of analysis, and will continue to be. For example in the area around the Merry Maidens in West Cornwall recent survey showed continuity from later prehistory through the medieval period to modern times in farming settlement and field system focus, but field-walking also found artefact scatters indicating settlement shifts in earlier prehistory (Johns and Herring 1995).

Elsewhere we have used the historic landscape character assessment to more effectively target evaluation and mitigation work before and during major developments. It has been especially useful in focusing geophysical work which has been directed towards comparing anciently and recently enclosed land, by testing assumptions regarding likely below ground components. Just a few modern agricultural drains were picked up in the recently enclosed land of Viverdon Downs in east Cornwall, while complex patterns of prehistoric

and medieval settlements, fields, and workplaces were recorded in anciently enclosed land near Probus, St Austell, and Trispen, all in advance of road improvements (Shiel 1994a and b; Shiel 1995; Gater 1996). Fluctuations in the margin of enclosed land were recorded at Callestick where a later prehistoric defended farming hamlet (a round) and an earlier prehistoric house were identified just beyond the present edge of an anciently-enclosed-land zone (Gater 1995). A major programme of archaeological recording on the A30 Indian Queens bypass (Rose, et al 1992) was designed with the likely differences between recently and anciently enclosed land in mind and again enhanced our knowledge of the character and components of the two zones. Boundaries sectioned were multi-phased in the anciently enclosed land, simple in the recently enclosed land; prehistoric and medieval settlement features were recorded in the anciently enclosed land, a prehistoric barrow and ritual area in the recently enclosed land, previously an area of open downland.

Projects like these provide new ideas for the map, text, and matrices which act as a type of research framework for future work. Virtually all archaeological work in Cornwall, past as well as present, provides useful input to the many explicit and implicit models which the framework contains, and it is hoped that all future archaeological work should make reference to the framework. Its use should not be confined to archaeological applications; document-based history will obtain models from the framework, as will ecology, and, of course, landscape architecture. All students of Cornwall, academic or otherwise, can dip into and feed back to the framework. In the process the applications and uses of the Cornwall historic landscape character assessment will multiply, and every time their results will feed back into our growing body of knowledge about the historic landscape. Application and use will increasingly be by people and bodies beyond Cornwall Archaeological Unit: planners, developers, countryside managers, historians, independent archaeologists, and members of the public. The results are to be fed into the County Planning Directorate's GIS as digitised maps. The character types and zones can then be viewed alongside other characterisations (and designations) on the system, as well of course as the Cornwall and Scilly SMR. The Isles of Scilly have also been successfully characterised using the Cornwall method, but at a larger scale (1:10,000). This was a project designed in the first place to inform the design of Countryside Stewardship proposals and agreements but the mapping will be of similar value to that for Cornwall (Land Use Consultants and Cornwall Archaeological Unit 1996).

We hope people will be critical of the material they work from, but that they also feel they own it. So far, we have had a good response from members of the public; people who know Cornwall, or parts of it, feel that the mapping works, that it represents and gives value to a Cornwall they can understand and recognise, and thus a Cornwall they want to conserve. It is important for them that the work indicates that all areas have historic character and value and therefore people who live in undesignated areas no longer feel that their homes are in some way second-class.

As suggested above, the mapping and the method which produced it, is perceived as being democratic and proper by ordinary people of Cornwall who have come into contact with it. It is not seen as being imposed by an expert but instead generated objectively and understandably from below, and from what is manifestly there, and which they can see from day to day. People are keen to see which zone they live in, what our present understanding of its history is, what sorts of components or features can be expected, and what we feel would be best for its future management. As people appear content with and excited by the mapping and text, the aim of in fluencing and educating is thus being achieved. We can only see this process accelerating as more people learn of and access the work. We are therefore optimistic about the effects of the Cornwall characterisation, because in the end, rather than achieve its conservation solely through constraint, protecting the past from the people, we would always prefer to persuade people to value, appreciate, and look after the historic landscape, thus allowing people to live in harmony with their heritage.

Acknowlegements

Peter Herring would like to thank Alison Farmer, Andrew Slater, and Prof Robert Tregay (Landscape Design Associates) and Graham Fairclough (English Heritage) for all their help and advice during the characterisation project. Nicholas Johnson (Cornwall County Archaeologist), Peter Rose, Steve Hartgroves, and Jeanette Ratcliffe helped and advised within Cornwall Archaeology Unit. Jenny McLynn word-processed the original document, the sense of which was improved by conversation with Trish Roberts and Cathy Parkes.

Annex 3: Definition of historic landscapes: 1993 Project brief for EH Historic Landscape Project

Introduction

1 It has been clear for many years that English Heritage cannot fully achieve its objectives of promoting the preservation of ancient monuments and historic buildings without a greater concern for the wider archaeological and historic environment in which individual monuments and buildings are set. In 1987, we published *Ancient monuments in the countryside* to emphasise the landscape context of archaeological sites. At the same time, we gained experience from preparing a register of historic parks and gardens. Finally, our assessment of complex areas of archaeological sites in our scheduling programme, in conjunction with increasing levels of co-operation and liaison with a wide range of countryside bodies, underlined the need to develop definitions and methodologies of assessment for ' the historic dimension of the landscape, particularly in the countryside. our first work on this was given added impetus by This common inheritance (DoE 1990), with its recognition of the importance of the historic landscape and its invitation to English Heritage to prepare a list of landscapes of historic importance.

2 Since 1990, English Heritage has published a preliminary policy statement and has issued a consultation paper to a wide range of national, local and professional bodies (Fairclough 1991, English Heritage 1991) Although there was little consensus on the form which any list of landscapes might take, responses to the consultation encouraged us to proceed with a series of small pilot projects to explore possible methodologies of historic landscape assessment. Although two of these are under-way (a small contribution to the Countryside Commission's Countryside Commission's *Countryside character maps* project (Countryside Commission forthcoming b) and, in co-operation with English Nature, work to explore the value of synthesising county sites and monuments data with nature conservation habitat surveys), the principal pilots have yet to be defined. We are seeking consultants' help in doing this, and in assessing the results. our longer-term aim is to select the most appropriate and robust methods of helping local authorities, landowners and other interested bodies to identify important areas of historic or archaeological interest in order to inform the allocation of countryside management resources.

3 Project objectives
3a The original objectives of this project were:

- i to identify, produce, tender documentation for, and manage a series of experimental research projects (pilot schemes) which will form the basis of the methodologies to be adopted for the definition of landscapes of historic importance

- ii to ensure that these pilot projects cover a diversity of circumstances (such as scale, location, agency, topography, land use)

- iii to draw together the results of the pilots in the form of a report comparing methodologies, approaches and results

3b Future objectives are:

- to make recommendations based on the results of 3a.iii for any further work considered necessary

- to prepare a draft manual defining and assessing historic landscapes for use by English Heritage

Tenderers should note that there is no guarantee that the successful consultant for 3(a) will be invited to tender for 3(b) or that 3(b) will proceed in the foreseeable future.

4 Scope of the project

For the purposes of this project, it will be accepted that the whole of the English landscape has been shaped largely by human use and activity. The historic components of the landscape are defined very broadly, ranging from the pattern of hedges, walls, fields, woodlands, and tracks which make up the skeleton of the landscape, to individual features such as archaeological sites, earthworks, historic buildings in farmsteads, hamlets, villages, and settlements. our present definition of the scope of historic landscapes is set out in our 1991 consultation paper. Semi-natural as well as archaeological, the ancient as well as the modern, industrial as well as pastoral are all dimensions which any definition must take into account.

5 We expect one or more practical, easily-used methodologies to emerge from the results of the pilots. Methodologies will need to be useable as a

working tool for the practical aspects of historic landscape conservation within the present countryside management and planning framework. An appropriate and workable methodology for defining and assessing landscapes of historic importance will follow three broad principles

- it will take account of all historical elements of the landscape, including semi-natural features such as hedges and woodland and sub-surface archaeological remains as well as the specific monuments and buildings more traditionally regarded as the historic dimension of the landscape

- it will allow the relative weighting, in robust and broad terms, of landscapes of greater or lesser historical depth and significance

- it will offer a method of evaluating individual features of a landscape as a guide for detailed day-to-day management by landowners, farmers and local conservation groups

6 Scope of pilot projects
We anticipate running between two and four pilot schemes within this project. However, the final number will depend on the number of schemes approved by the Steering Group and English Heritage. For tendering purposes, consultants are to assume that a minimum of four schemes must be submitted at stage 1 for consideration by the Steering Group. The consultant may submit additional schemes with the approval of the project manager, up to a maximum of six schemes.

The pilot schemes are required to explore a range of approaches to define landscapes of historic importance taking into consideration English Heritages 1991 Consultation Paper. In particular, the pilot schemes should aim to test the appropriateness of different

- scales (regional, county or more local as the basic area for assessment)

- source material (including SMR information, nature conservation and landscape records, documentary and cartographic evidence for later periods, air and satellite photography, field survey, published information

- agency (it is intended to run pilots, carried out in a variety of organisational and professional contexts for example local authority, environmental consultant or university using a range of professions, eg archaeologists, landscape historians, and historic geographers)

- methods of measuring importance and of classification

- perspectives (how to reconcile individual elements of a landscape with its whole whether 'top-down' on a regional or typological basis or 'bottom-up' by accreting individual components)

- location (it is intended to explore regional contrasts and character by examining different parts of England).

7 Programme of work
The project has five principal stages, with in-built review, authorisation, and monitoring at each stage by English Heritage. The satisfactory completion of each stage will be confirmed by the Steering Group before the consultant proceeds to the next stage.

- **Stage 1**: identification and presentation of suitable pilot projects, taking into account the detailed objectives in paragraphs 5 and 6 and any other issues which the consultant or the project manager may reasonably consider appropriate.

- **Stage 2**: preparation of outline specifications for the approved pilot schemes. Presentation of outline specification to the Steering Group for their approval.

- **Stage 3**: Preparation of tender documentation including conditions of contract and detailed specification for pilot schemes for approval by English Heritage. Advertising and making recommendations for the tender list. Evaluation of tenders and make recommendations for the Steering Group on the selection of consultant for each pilot scheme.

Note: Unless otherwise agreed in writing by the Project manager, all pilot schemes will be undertaken by other consultants who will be commissioned directly by English Heritage.

- **Stage 4:** Management of pilot schemes including supervision and monitoringto ensure consultants complying with the specification and programme. Certification of consultants invoices for payment by English Heritage which should be passed to the project manager within five days of receipt. Reports at agreed intervals to project manager on progressof pilot projects which should detail any problems or delays affecting the completion of thescheme.

- **Stage 5:** Comparative analysis of methods tested by pilot projects and of their results, culminating in recommendations for appropriate methodologies, probably in the form of a statement of options.

Bibliography

Berry, A Q, and Brown, I W, 1995 *Managing ancient monuments – an integrated approach* Clywd Archaeol Services and Assoc County Archaeol Officers

Brandon, P, and Millman, R (eds), 1978 *Historic landscapes identification, recording and management* Proc conference at Polytechnic of North London

CLRAE, 1998 *Draft European Landscape Convention* (Congress of Local and Regional Authorities in Europe, Strasbourg)

Cadw, 1998 *Register of landscapes of outstanding historic interest in Wales* (Register, pt 2.1), Cardiff

CRC and OAU, 1993 Cobham Resource Consultants, Oxford Archaeol Unit, and English Heritage *Historic landscapes project* typescript report to English Heritage

Cole, R, 1996 *An archaeological assessment of Carland Cross to Trispen, A39 road development* Cornwall Archaeol Unit (Cornwall County Council)

Colley, R, and Lee, N, 1990 Reviewing the quality of environmental statements *The Planner* **76.16** April, 12–13

Coones, P, 1985 One landscape or many? A geographical perspective *Landscape History* 7 5–12

Cornwall County Council, 1996 *Cornwall landscape assessment 1994* report prepared for the Countryside Commission by Landscape Design Associates and Cornwall Archaeol Unit (Cornwall County Council) Truro

Cosgrove, D 1990 Landscape studies in geography and cognate fields of the humanities and social sciences *Landscape Research* **15.3** 1–6

Council of Europe, 1995 *Recommendation No R(95)9 of the Committee of Ministers to Member States on the integrated conservation of cultural landscape areas as part of landscape policies* Strasbourg

—, 1996 *Helsinki Declaration* MAC 4(96)1rev

Countryside Agency, 1999 *Countryside Character*
vol 4 *East Midlands* (CA 10)
vol 5 *West Midlands* (CA 11)
vol 6 *The East* (CA 12)
vol 7 *South East* (CA 13)
vol 8 *South West* (CA 14)

Countryside Commision 1990 *The Cotswold landscape – a landscape assessment* (CCP294) Cheltenham

—, 1993 *Landscape assessment guidance* (CCP423) Cheltenham

—, 1994a *Views from the past – historic landscape character in the English countryside* (consultation document) Cheltenham

—, 1994b *The new map of England – a celebration of the south west landscape* (CCP444) Cheltenham

—, 1994c *The landscape of Bodmin Moor*, report by Land Use Consultants and Cornwall Archaeol Unit (Cornwall County Council) Cheltenham

—, 1994d *Cornwall, a landscape assessment*

—, 1994e *Historic landscape assessment, the development of a methodology*

—, 1996 *Views from the past – historic landscape character in the English countryside* (CCW4) Cheltenham

—, 1998a *Landscape assessment of the Cornwall Area of Outstanding Natural Beauty* report by Landscape Design Associates

—, 1998b *Countryside Character*
vol 1 *North East* (CCP 535)
vol 2 *North West* (CCP 536)
vol 3 *Yorkshire and the Humber* (CCP 537)

—, English Heritage, and English Nature 1993 *Conservation issues in strategic plans* (CCP420) Cheltenham

—, —, and —, 1997 *What matters and why environmental capital – a new approach* Cheltenham

Coupe, M, and Fairclough, G J, 1991 Protection for the historic and natural landscape *Landscape Design* **201** Jun, 24–30

Darvill, T, 1987 *Ancient monuments in the countryside: an archaeological management review* English Heritage (HBMC) report 5

—, Gerrard, C, and Startin, B, 1993 Identifying and protecting historic landscapes *Antiquity* **67.256** 563–74

—, Saunders, A, and Startin, B, 1987 A question of national importance: approaches to the evaluation of ancient monuments for the Monuments Protection Programme in England *Antiquity* **61.233** 393–408

DoE, 1973 Planning Circ 23/77 *Historic buildings and conservation areas*

—, 1988 *European Union environmental impact assessment directive* Planning Circ 15/88

—, 1989 *Environmental assessment: a guide to the procedures*

—, 1990 *This common inheritance* White Paper, HMSO

—, 1991 *Planning policy guidance note 16 Archaeology and planning*, (PPG-16) HMSO

—, 1994a *UK action plan for biodiversity* HMSO (Cmd 2428)

—, 1994b *Sustainable development the UK strategy* HMSO (Cmd 2426)

—, and DNH, 1994 *Planning policy guidance note 15, Planning and the historic environment* (PPG-15) HMSO

English Heritage, 1990 The man-made and natural environments *Conservation Bull* **12**, 5–7

—,1991a Planning for parks and gardens *Conservation Bull* **13**, 12–13

—, 1991b *Exploring our past: strategies for the archaeology of England*

—, 1991c *Golf course proposals in historic landscapes*

—, 1991d *Register of landscapes of historic importance, a consultation paper*

—, 1992 *Development plan policies for archaeology* English Heritage advice note

—, 1997a *Sustaining the historic environment: new perspectives on the future, an English Heritage discussion document*

—, 1997b *The Monuments Protection Programme 1986–96 in retrospect*

—, Countryside Commission, and English Nature, 1996 *Conservation issues in local plans*

English Nature, 1997–8 *Natural areas profiles* (many volumes, available from English Nature local teams)

—, 1998 *Natural areas profiles* (CD-Rom)

Essex County Council, 1992 *The Essex guide to environmental assessment* Essex Planning Officers Assoc, Essex County Council

Everitt, A , 1986 *Continuity and colonization, the evolution of Kentish settlement* Leicester University Press

Fairclough, G J, 1991 The historic landscape, an English Heritage policy statement, *Conservation Bull* **14**, 4–5

—, 1992 Meaningful constructions – spatial and functional analysis of medieval buildings *Antiquity* **66.251** 348–66

—, 1994a *Landscapes from the past – only human nature*, in Selman 1994, 64–72

—, 1994b *Recent work in England – English Heritage* in ICOMOS 1994b, 31–8

—, 1995 *The sum of all its parts, an overview of the politics of integrated management in England* in Berry, and Brown, 1995, 17–28

—, 1998 Assessment and characterisation: EH's historic landscape policy, in *Landscapes perception, recognition and management: reconciling the impossible?* Proc of a conference at Sheffield, 1996 (Landscape archaeology and ecology vol 3), The Landscape Conservation Forum and Sheffeld Hallam University), 43–51

—, 1999a Protecting time and space: understanding historic landscape for conservation in England, in Ucko, P J, and Layton, R, 1999: *The archaeology and anthropology of landscape: shaping your landscape* (Proc of the World Archaeology Congress, New Delhi, 1994), One World Archaeology **30**, Routledge, London, 119–34

—, 1999b *Historic landscape assessment in England: a summary of work to date sponsored by English Heritage* in Macinnes, (ed), 1999, 9–14

—, (ed) 1999c *Historic landscape characterisation; the state of the art* papers from an English Heritage seminar at the Soc of Antiqu, London, 11 December 1998, 3–14

—,1999d Protecting the cultural landscape – national designations and local character in Grenville, J, (ed), *Managing the historic rural landscape*

—, forthcoming Place and locality a non-monumental heritage? in *Proc of the Interpreting Historic Places Conference, York, 3–7 September 1997*, Routledge

Gater, J, 1995 *Cornwall spine main, Engelly to Sevenmilestone: report on geophysical survey* Geophysical Surveys of Bradford

—, 1996 *A3076 Trispen Bypass: report on geophysical survey* Geophysical Surveys of Bradford

Gerrard, S, 1997, *English Heritage book of Dartmoor*

Goodchild, P H, 1990 *Some principles for the conservation of historic landscapes* presented to ICOMOS(UK) Historic Gardens and Landscapes Committee

Heaney, D, and Therivel, R, 1993 *Directory of environmental statements 1988–92* Oxford Brookes University

Herring, P C, 1992 *St Michael's Mount, an archaeological assessment* Cornwall Archaeol Unit (Cornwall County Council) and English Heritage, Truro

—, 1998 *Cornwall's historic landscape: presenting a method of historic landscape assessment* Cornwall Archaeol Unit (Cornwall County Council) and English Heritage, Truro

—, and Johnson, N, 1999 *Landscape characterisation: the Cornwall study* in Macinnes 1999, 15–26

—, and Smith, J R, 1991 *The archaeology of the St Austell china clay area* Cornwall Archaeol Unit (Cornwall County Council), Truro

—, and Thomas, S N H, 1990 *Kit Hill, an archaeological survey* Cornwall Archaeol Unit (Cornwall County Council), Truro

Hoskins, W G, 1955 *The making of the English landscape*

ICOMOS UK 1994a, *World Heritage Site guidelines for the landscape* (UNESCO)

—, 1994b *Proc of seminar on cultural landscapes* at Soc of Antiqu, London, 23 June, 1994

Johanssen, B O H, 1994 *Council of Europe draft recommendations on the integrated conservation of cultural landscape areas* in ICOMOS UK, 1994b, 39–46

Jones, M, and Rotherham, I D, (eds), 1998 *Landscapes: perception, recognition and management: reconciling the impossible?* Proc of a Landscape Conservation Forum conference, Sheffield, April 1996 (Landscape archaeology and ecology, vol 3, Sheffield)

Johns, C, and Herring, P C, 1995 *The Tregothnan Estate, Penwith, an archaeological assessment* Cornwall Archaeol Unit (Cornwall County Council), Truro

—, and —, 1996 *St Keverne historic landscape assessment* Cornwall Archaeol Unit (Cornwall County Council), Truro

Johnson, N D, 1998 Cornish farms in prehistoric farmyards *British Archaeol* **31** February, 12–13

—, and Rose, P G, 1994 *Bodmin Moor, an archaeological survey: vol I the human landscape to c1800* English Heritage Archaeol rep 24 and RCHME Sup Ser 11

Jones, C, 1992 *UK EAs 1991: a comparative analysis* EIA Centre, Manchester University Occ Pap 36

—, Lee, N, and Wood, C, 1991 *UK environmental statements 1988–90 an analysis* EIA Centre, Manchester University Occ Pap 29

Keen, L, and Carreck, L, 1987 *Historic landscape of the Weld Estate* Dorset County Council unpublished

Kelly, R, 1993 *Register of landscapes, parks and gardens of special historic interest in Wales* unpubl Cadw discussion paper

—, 1994 *Interim report on first years work, 1993–4 towards producing a list of historic landscapes in Wales* Cadw/Countryside Commission for Wales/ICOMOS UK

Kent County Council, nd *Kent Environmental Assessment handbook*

—, 1983 *Countryside Local Plan written statement* Kent County Council

—, 1992a *The historic parks and gardens of Kent* A comprehensive survey of the most significant historic parks and gardens in Kent, Kent County Council Planning Dept and Kent Gardens Trust (vol 1: A to J, vol 2: K to Z)

—, 1992b *The Kent garden compendium* A comprehensive register of gardens of historic, horticultural, amenity or other value in the County of Kent (vol 1: main text; vol 2: gardens maps)

—, 1993 *Draft landscape and nature conservation guidelines* Kent County Council

Lambrick, G, 1985 *Archaeology and nature conservation* Oxford University Dept for External Studies

—, 1992a *The importance of the cultural heritage in a green world towards the development of landscape integrity assessment* in Macinnes, and Wickham-Jones, (eds), 1992, 105–26

—, 1992b Environment assessment and the historic environment, principles, practice and problems in *Advances in environment assessment*, Conference Oct 1992, IEA

—, 1993 *Environmental assessment and the cultural heritage principles and practice* in Ralston and Thomas 1993, 9–19

—, and Bramhill, P, 1999 *Hampshire historic landscape asessment* Oxford Archaeol Unit and Scott Wilson, for Hampshire County Council, 2 vols

Landscape Design Associates (LDA) and Cornwall Archaeol Unit (CAU), 1994 *Historic landscape assessment: a methodological case-study in Cornwall* (draft report for English Heritage and the Countryside Commison)

Landscape Practice with Martin Stancliffe Architects, 1992 *Plumpton Rocks* unpubl client report

Landscape Research Group, 1988 *A review of recent practice and research in landscape assessment* Countryside Commission (CCP25)

Land Use Consultants, 1991 *River landscape assessment methodology* for National Rivers Authority, Severn Trent Region

—, and Cornwall Archaeological Unit, 1996 *Isles of Scilly historic landscape assessment and management strategy* report to The Duchy of Cornwall, Countryside Commission, and MAFF

Larsen, S E, 1992 Is nature really natural *Landscape research* **17.3** 116–22

Lee, N, and Colley, R, 1990 *Reviewing the quality of environmental statements* EIA Centre, Manchester University Occ Pap 24

Lloyd, R, 1994 *Recent work in England, the Countryside Commission* in ICOMOS UK, 1994b 17–23

MAFF and English Heritage, 1992 *Farming, historic landscapes and people*

Macinnes, L, 1994 *The historic landscape in Scotland* ICOMOS UK, 1994b, 2–30

—, (ed), 1999 *Assessing cultural landscapes: progress and potential* Proc of a seminar in Longmore House, Edinburgh, February 1998, ICOMOS UK, Edinburgh

—, and Wickham-Jones, C R, 1992 *All natural things archaeology and the Green debate* Oxbow Mono 21

Miller, K, 1999 *Using Historic Landscape Characterisation for land management in the Isle of Axholme project*, in Fairclough 1999c, 91–112

Morgan Evans, D, 1985 *The management of historic landscapes* in Lambrick, 1985, 89–94

National Trust, 1990 *Great Langdale vol 1: history of land use* unpubl internal report

—, 1992 *Archaeological and historic landscape survey; guidelines for data collection and compilation* unpubl internal guide

Nature Conservancy Council 1990 *Handbook for phase 1, habitat survey* England Field Unit, English Nature, Peterborough

Rackham, O, 1986, *The history of the countryside*

Ralston, I, and Thomas, R, (eds) 1993 *Environmental assessment and archaeology* IFA Occ Pap 5

Ratcliffe, J, 1989 *The archaeology of the Isles of Scilly and its management* Cornwall Archaeol Unit (Cornwall County Council), Truro

Roberts, B K, and Wrathmell, S, 1995 *Terrain and rural settlement mapping: the methodology and preliminary results* Durham University Geography Dept Rep Services

—, and —, forthcoming *Atlas of land settlement in England* English Heritage

Rose, P G, Herring, P C, and Nowakowski, JA, 1992 *The A30 Fraddon to Indian Queens improvement, recommendations for archaeological recording* Cornwall Archaeol Unit (Cornwall County Council), Truro

Russett, V, 1988 *The Manor of Widcombe: an historic landscape survey* Avon County Council unpublished

Selman, P, (ed) 1994 *The ecology and management of cultural landscapes* Proc of the Internat Assoc of Landscape Ecologists (UK Branch) 1993 Conference Cultural Landscapes' in *Landscape Issues,* J of the Dept of Countryside and Landscape, Cheltenham **11.1**

Shanks, M, 1993 *Experiencing the past* Routledge, London

Shiel, D, 1994a *Probus bypass: report on geophysical survey* Geophysical Surveys of Bradford

—, 1994b A388 *Viverdon Down: report on geophysical survey* Geophysical Surveys of Bradford

—, 1995 *St Austell North-east distributor road: report on geophysical survey* Geophysical Surveys of Bradford

Smith, J R, 1988 *The Luxulyan Valley report* Cornwall Archaeol Unit (Cornwall County Council), Truro

Strutt and Parker, nd *Part Firle estate management plan* unpubl client report

Swanwick, C, 1989 People, nature and landscape, a research review *Landscape Research* **14.3** 3–7

Thomas, S N H, 1992 *The archaeology of the Trevu to St Erth water main* Cornwall Archaeol Unit (Cornwall County Council), Truro

—, 1994 *Lanhydrock, an archaeological assessment* Cornwall Archaeol Unit, (Cornwall County Council), Truro

—, 1996 *An archaeological assessment of the Sevenmilestone to North Country water main* Cornwall Archaeol Unit (Cornwall County Council), Truro

—, and Johns, C, 1995 *An archaeological evaluation of the St Austell North-east distributor road* Cornwall Archaeol Unit (Cornwall County Council), Truro

—, and Rose, PG, 1990 *An archaeological assessment of the Kit Hill to St Mellion water main* Cornwall Archaeol Unit (Cornwall County Council), Truro

Wägenbaum, T, 1993 *The construction of nature* Working pap 20 of the 'Man and Nature' Humanities Research Centre, Odense University

Wallenberg, J K, 1931 *Kentish place-names: a topographical and etymological study of the place-name material in Kentish charters dated before the Conquest*

—, 1934 *The place-names of Kent*

Wood, C, and Jones, C, 1991 *Monitoring environmental assessment and planning* HMSO